Huston-Tillotson University Research Journal

Inaugural Edition

authorHOUSE®

AuthorHouse™
1663 Liberty Drive, Suite 200
Bloomington, IN 47403
www.authorhouse.com
Phone: 1-800-839-8640

First published by AuthorHouse 6/26/2007

ISBN: 978-1-4343-0484-1 (sc)

Printed in the United States of America
Bloomington, Indiana

This book is printed on acid-free paper.

THE INAUGURAL EDITION OF THE HUSTON-TILLOTSON UNIVERSITY RESEARCH JOURNAL has as its goal the dissemination of research presentations prepared and presented by Huston-Tillotson University students at the Huston-Tillotson University Inaugural Student Research Day on April 25, 2006.

THE HUSTON-TILLOTSON UNIVERSITY RESEARCH JOURNAL will be published annually for Huston-Tillotson University, 900 Chicon Street, Austin, Texas 78702.

HUSTON-TILLOTSON UNIVERSITY
RESEARCH JOURNAL: INAUGURAL EDITION
CONTENTS

LETTER FROM THE PRESIDENT

The inaugural Huston-Tillotson Research Day 2006 and this student research publication represent a reinvigoration of the University's historical legacy of empirical investigation. HT holds the distinction of being the oldest institution of higher education in Central Texas with a complementary historical distinction for promoting scientific inquiry and research.

The University's historical reputation for empirical research is exemplified by the late James Harris Jr., an HT graduate, whose contributions to the field of scholarly research are highlighted in this publication. Mr. Harris's story represents only one of many HT graduates whose outstanding contributions to the field of research must be extricated from long forgotten archives.

It is the intent of the inaugural research day to serve as a precedent with future Student Research Day activities to feature other HT graduates who have made noteworthy empirical research contributions. Reclaiming this rich legacy can provide more tangible role models for students and as such, provide an even greater impetus for them to pursue research in their own areas of interest. Furthermore, the opportunity that this day dedicated to student research and the publication of results affords, in terms of jumpstarting the careers of those who may walk in the footsteps of James Harris, cannot be underestimated.

Larry L. Earvin, Ph.D.
President and CEO

FOREWORD

Huston-Tillotson University (HT) inaugurated Research Day in 2005/06. This milestone event culminated in the Huston-Tillotson University Research Journal which contains papers presented by students at the Research Day program. Although this research journal is a "first" for HT, an outstanding antecedent to the Journal was the pioneering research leading to the discovery of elements 104 and 105 and publications by the Albert Ghiorso team at Stanford University which included James Harris, Jr., an HT chemistry graduate, who was employed by the U. S. Atomic Energy Commission and published his co-discovery of two radioactive elements during the 1970's. In the previous decade, other African Americans made significant contributions in social action research where, for the first time in history, social science research was used to impact a Supreme Court case, resulting in the landmark Brown vs. the Board of Education decision that ushered in the desegregation/civil rights movement. Current research at HT continues the traditions of James Harris, Jr. and Drs. Kenneth and Mamie Clark.

In this issue of the Huston-Tillotson University Research Journal, several papers focus on social research involving health disparities in underserved communities surrounding HT. A poignant example of this problem is presented in a study by an HT student documenting the misdiagnosis of ailments in Hispanic and other racial/ethnic minority groups. Another article reveals a comparative analysis of communitarian societies with virtual communities which are social interaction networks that have been reinvented through cyberspace frameworks. Social action research by students is shown, further, in a paper that focuses on the social structure of our society and how it translates into punitive behavior toward the least powerful and on the potential mental health of female athletes.

Huston-Tillotson students in business analyzed internal control assessment filing of financial processes in corporate America and raised issues about the Sarbanes-Oxley Act (SOX) implementation scheme. Other papers presented at the Research Day program focused on opinions about religious diversity.

This inaugural issue of the Huston-Tillotson University Research Journal reveals a broad spectrum of studies by HT students and their faculty advisers and epitomizes a goal of the University which is to encourage student learning through inquiry and discovery. Therefore, the Research Day Committee and the student presenters/writers are commended for bringing this publication to fruition and setting a high standard of scholarship which future writers must emulate.

Joseph Jones, Jr. Ph.D.
Dean, College of Arts and Sciences

I. Historical Papers

Heavy Ion Accelerators: History and Controversy

Richard Northcote
Sophomore, Chemistry

Dr. Muchere C. Russ, Major Advisor for Chemistry

Abstract

Uranium (Atomic Number = 92) was once thought to be the end of all possible elements. For 120 years Uranium was the last element on the periodic table, until 1940 when neptunium was discovered by nuclear bombardment. Once it had been confirmed that there was an element heavier than uranium, even if it was made synthetically, the race was on to discover new heavy elements and isotopes. In order to make these new discoveries, new theories and technology would have to be produced. The first Cyclotron was built at the University of California, Berkeley and quickly became the hub of nuclear research. Heavy Ion Linear Accelerators (HILAC) were born from the limitations of the early cyclotrons. Cyclotrons could only capture 10% of the beam generated for bombardment of nuclei, while HILAC because of their linearity could capture 100% of the beam because there was no energy lost to the curvature. At the University of California at Berkeley, Albert Ghiorso led a team of research scientists including Huston-Tillotson alumnus James A. Harris, in the discovery of trans-uranium elements 104 and 105. Not realized at the time, the break-through research conducted with the HILAC would change modern medicine and the nuclear community. As well, an international naming debate was instigated.

History and Background

Uranium, named after the planet Uranus, is the heaviest naturally occurring element found on earth. Uranium is a heavy metal, 65% more dense than lead. Uranium will react with cold water and reacts with air to form uranium oxide, a blackish metallic compound and the most common form of Uranium. Uranium is designated by the symbol, U, in the periodic table of the elements (Figure 1.). It was not officially known until 1789, when Klaproth isolated it from pitchblende [1]. However, as early as 79 C.E., the oxide of uranium, U_3O_8, was used by glass makers to give glass a yellow color (Figure 2).

In 1896, Uranium was found to have radioactive properties when Henri Becquerel wrapped a lump of uranium in a black cloth, left it on top of some film to be exposed in sunlight, then noted that the film showed signs of exposure before he even took it outside. This led him to investigate the spontaneous emission of nuclear radiation and he was later awarded the 1903 Nobel Prize for his discovery [2]. Radioactivity is the spontaneous emission of a subatomic particle from a nucleus. Radioactive decay happens when an unstable nucleus releases a subatomic particle to form a more stable smaller nucleus. This radioactive property led chemists to wonder if uranium was in fact a daughter of a larger element that decayed to form uranium. This was the first effort to try and find or theorize the existence of trans-uranium elements: elements larger than uranium.

After radioactivity was discovered, the next great discovery was the neutron. Discovered in 1930, the neutron is a subatomic particle with no net charge and a mass of 1.6749 atomic mass units, slightly heavier than a proton [3]. With this discovery, the understanding of the nucleus increased significantly. It was then theorized by Otto Hahn in 1933 that maybe if uranium was bombarded with a beam of neutrons new isotopes and possibly new elements could be made. In 1934 in Rome this theory was tested by E. Fermi, E. Amaldi, O. D'Agostino, F. Rasetti, and E. Segerè. They bombarded uranium in a glass tube in a vacuum with neutrons and obtained a series of β-particle-emitting radioactive products. They named these products 23-minute products due to their 23-minute activity period. However, they were not found to be new elements. Segerè concluded that trans-uranium elements were not possible [4].

In 1931, the first cyclotron was built from the plans of Ernest O. Lawrence and M. Stanley Livingston at the University of California, Berkeley [4]. The cyclotron is a monstrous structure (Figure 3.), making a complete ring to spin a particle in cycles. The cyclotron was made to accelerate particles near light speed to bombard a target or a purified element. The cyclotron works by amplifying a current through a particle to give it a charge, creating an ion. The ion is then directed through a magnetic field to push and pull the particle in a direction. A powerful magnet changes the charge from positive to negative as the particle approaches and leaves a magnet in the ring. This transition attracts and repels the particle; thus giving the particle a constant acceleration while holding it in the magnetic field.

In 1939, Edwin M. McMillan began to think that the Segerè conclusions were wrong. He postulated that the 23-minute uranium product might be a daughter product of uranium and be element-93 with an atomic weight of 239. In the spring of 1940, he was able to separate, identify, and thus discover element-93 after bombarding uranium with neutrons in the cyclotron. McMillan's findings confirmed that it was possible to create elements with higher atomic numbers than uranium. Further research showed that an increase of energy yielded different isotopes, the most stable being element237-93, where 93 is the atomic number or number of protons in the nucleus and 237 is the atomic weight. Element237-93 would later be named Neptunium, after Neptune, the next planet after Uranus [4]. Later in December of 1940, uranium was bombarded in the cyclotron with deuterons – a positively charged particle consisting of a proton and a neutron, equivalent to the nucleus of an atom of deuterium – was used to yield an element with an atomic number of 94 and a half-life of 50 years; later element237-94 was prepared, with a half-life of 24,000 years. This latter element was named Plutonium, after Pluto, the last known planet in the solar system and this year it has been demoted from planet status to dwarf planet.

Improving the Cyclotron

In 1952, all elements up to 100 had been discovered and reconstructed in the 60-inch cyclotron (refer to Figure 3). In 1952, the limitations of the cyclotrons were realized and a new technique was required to produce new elements. However, it was clear that the cyclotron was inefficient at producing the particle beams necessary for heavy ion acceleration, that is, ions heavier than hydrogen. Only ten percent of the original beam could be captured due to a phenomenon of electrons loosing energy as they travel through an arc, also called synchrotron radiation. The solution was development of the Linear Accelerator (Figure 4.). The Linear Accelerator (LINAC) could capture 100 percent of the particle beam and could accelerate particles heavier than hydrogen to atom-smashing speeds, that is, close to the speed of light. A "heavy" ion is a charged atom with two or more protons in its nucleus, which means every element on the periodic table from helium on up. The LINAC was one of the first machines that could accelerate elements as heavy as argon (atomic mass of 40) with "atom-smashing" energies. Once again, construction for the LINAC began at the University of California, Berkeley [5].

The Huston-Tillotson Connection

Albert Ghiorso led research to discover more heavy elements using the new linear accelerator capable of accelerating heavy particles (HILAC). His team included Nurmia, K. A. Y. Eskola, P. L. Eskola, and Huston-Tillotson alumnus James Andrew Harris (Figure 5.). Harris was the first African American to participate in a major new-element identification program and co-discoverer of elements 104 and 105. He was born on March 26, 1932 in Waco, Texas. After earning a B.S. in chemistry at Huston-Tillotson in Austin, Texas, Harris served in the army. After he completed his service,

he joined Tracerlab, Inc. in Richmond, California. At Tracerlab he worked as a chemist for five years. In 1960, Harris left Tracerlab to accept a position in the Nuclear Chemistry Division of the Lawrence Radiation Laboratory at the University of California, Berkeley. He became part of the team that discovered and identified elements 104 and 105 in 1969-1970. His job was to create the highly pure targets used in the identification of element-104 and element-105 [6]. He did all chemical separations and purifications of the targets for bombardment; these targets included highly purified californium and uranium. In a press release at the time, his colleague and research leader Albert Ghiorso stated that James Harris created "the best target that has ever been available for heavy-element research" [7].

In 1969, the team had a break through and discovered the first transactinide element, or the first super-heavy element with an atomic number of 104. To do this, they bombarded californium-249 (^{249}Cf) with nuclei from carbon-12 (^{12}C) of 71 MeV and ^{13}C nuclei with 69 MeV. 1 MeV is equivalent to 1.602 x 10^{-13} Joules; 3.2×10^{-11} Joules or 200 MeV is equal to total energy released in nuclear fission of one U-235 atom on average. This combination spontaneously emitted four electrons to form element257-104. The isotope had a half life of 4 to 5 seconds and decayed by emitting an α-particle to form Nobelium-255. An α-particle is a highly ionized low penetration form of radiation with two protons and two neutrons, He^{2+}. Element 259-104 is formed by the merging of a ^{13}C nuclei with ^{249}Cf, followed by emission of three neutrons. This isotope has a half-life of 3 to 4 s and decays by emitting an alpha particle into Nobelium253, which has a half-life of 105 s. The Berkeley group was able to successfully repeat the process using the LINAC and since the discovery of element 104 thousands of atoms of 257-104 and 259-104 have been detected [8].

Element 105 was discovered in April 1970 by the Berkeley group. The discovery was made by bombarding a target of ^{249}Cf with a beam of 84 MeV nitrogen (^{15}N) nuclei in the HILAC. In October 1971, it was announced that two new isotopes of Element 105 were synthesized with the linear accelerator by A. Ghiorso and co-workers at Berkeley[9]. Element105 was produced both by bombarding Californium-250 with ^{15}N and by bombarding Berkelium-249 with Oxygen-18 atoms. The isotope, ^{261}Rf emits 8.93-MeV alpha particles and decays to Lawrencium-257 with a half-life of about 1.8 s. And the second isotope, ^{262}Rf, produced by bombarding Berkelium-249 with oxygen, emits 8.45 MeV alpha particles and decays to Lawrencium-258 with a half-life of about 40 s.

Naming Crisis

The Berkeley group proposed the names Rutherfordium for element-104, in honor of Ernest Rutherford, a pioneering New Zealand Physicist, and Hahnium for element-105 after the early nuclear chemist Otto Hahn. However, the Berkeley group was not the only party with claims to these discoveries or what the names of these new elements should be. A Soviet team working at the Joint Institute for Nuclear Research at Dubna, U.S.S.R., referred to as the Dubna group, claimed to have discovered element-104 in 1967. The Dubna group also claimed to have found element-105 in April 1970, close to the same time as the Berkeley group. The Dubna group claimed to have bombarded plutonium (Pu) with accelerated 113-115 MeV neon ions. By measuring fission tracks in a special glass with a microscope, they detected an isotope that decays by spontaneous fission. The Soviets proposed this reaction: Pu + Ne → element104 + 4 neutrons + Pu + Ne. The Berkeley team attempted to reproduce element-104 using the Dubna group's methods with more sophisticated equipment such as the LINAC without any success [10]. The Berkeley group also attempted to construct isotopes of element-105 from the Dubna research group process by bombarding Americium-243 with Neon-22 to produce element261-105. Once again, the Berkeley group could not reproduce the products [11]. Glenn Seaborg, 1951 Nobel Laureate for his role in the discovery of several trans-uranium elements, even went so far as to suggest that the Soviets falsified the discovery [12]. This was the beginning of the international naming debate.

The Berkeley group argued that the Dubna group must have mistakenly identified these new elements, since no one outside the Dubna group could reproduce the Dubna results. The Soviet Dubna team argued that they had produced the element and the Americans just could not replicate the process. To settle this process the International Union of Pure and Applied Chemistry (IUPAC) proposed that a Dubna representative go to Berkeley, a Berkeley representative travel to the U.S.S.R, and also a neutral scientist from Germany would accompany both. Both groups agreed to this, but the exchange never took place. In 1994, the IUPAC tried to overcome this dispute by naming element-104, dubnium, after the Dubna group and element-105, joliotium. This was not accepted by either side. Finally in 1997, the following names were agreed to: 104-rutherfordium and 105-dubnium [13].

Medical Advancement

Despite the controversy over elemental naming, one thing is certain; the introduction of the LINAC and cyclotrons into scientific research has made it possible for modern medicine to advance beyond imagination. Different isotopes of common elements like iodine were produced in the cyclotrons and HILAC. The investigation into radiation started an interdisciplinary effort with a special emphasis on medicine. One of the driving forces for higher currents and higher energies was the demand for radiosodium to treat patients. Early on when the discovery that 90 percent of a cyclotron beam is lost, Robert Wilson and Martin Kamen devised probes to capture some of the lost energy. They would skim off the lost beam with probes made of ferrous phosphide; this would make ^{32}P and ^{59}Fe for use by both physicists and biologists. This ingenious move tripled the effectiveness of their research. (1) The new isotope of iron could be used in the research of hemoglobin in the blood stream. This element allowed for tremendous advances in blood formation and dynamics and the management of various blood diseases. (2) The discovery in the HILAC of cobalt-60, with a half life of around 5.3 years, is now used in the therapeutic irradiation of over 4,000,000 patients in the United States each year. (3)Possibly the most important discovery with the HILAC was Seaborg's discovery of Iodine-131, which is now used in some two million cases of treatment of thyroid disease. Iodine-131 is also used for diagnosing of kidney and liver disorders, in finding brain tumors, and to determine blood and plasma volume. The uses for Iodine-131 go on and on. Furthermore, ninety-nine percent of all nuclear medical research uses ^{131}I [14].

New Energy Forms

Four important forms of energy production have resulted while researching the cyclotrons and LINAC. The first is nuclear fission. Nuclear fission occurs when an element splits into two smaller nuclei. This emits massive amounts of radiation and, in close proximity, will cause a nuclear chain reaction where one atom splitting and the emitting radiation collides with another atom causing that atom to split (Figure 6.). As this process continues the energy produces the explosive power of the nuclear bomb or consumer energy in a controlled process of a nuclear power plant. The second form is fusion. Fusion is the process of fusing two nuclei together to form a single nucleus (Figure 7). Fusion happens at extremely high temperatures and has a tendency for elements of lower atomic number than iron to release energy, while elements larger than iron absorb energy. This is used in thermonuclear warheads where a nuclear explosion generates enough heat to fuse hydrogen nuclei together releasing almost 100 times more explosive power than a traditional fission nuclear weapon and heats hotter than the surface of the sun [15]. Thirdly, cold fusion was later explored. Cold fusion is the combining of nuclei at temperatures far below those of thermonuclear reactions. Cold fusion looks promising as a means of generating huge amounts of energy with little waste product. However, cold fusion is highly controversial, since again the 1989 alleged discovery has yet to be reproduced in a controlled manner. Fourthly, the most powerful form of energy is antimatter. Antimatter is matter composed of antiparticles, essentially subatomic particles with opposite traditional charges, i.e., negative protons and positive electrons (Figure 8). Antimatter can be described as the parallel to matter or a reflection of matter that is opposite in every sense (Figure 9). If a matter particle and an antimatter particle contact each other they annihilate each other with a burst of energy or electromagnetic radiation. In these reactions, rest matter is not conserved, but $E = mc^2$ (Einstein's theory of relativity) is conserved. Production of anti-matter was made effective in the 1990's and there is talk of harnessing anti-matter for propulsion in space travel due to its enormous energy potential [16]. The HILAC is very effective in reproducing these reactions and is one of the primary sources in the formation of antimatter energy [17].

Summary

The research that started with the quest for trans-uranium elements has had farther reaching effects than the expansion of the periodic table of the elements. There are twenty percent more known elements now in the periodic table as a result of the research for heavy elements. Nuclear power is a relatively cheap and cleaner solution than conventional power supplies. Weapons of last resort keep the worlds major powers from fighting tragic wars and promoted a technology race that has lead to the exploration of the heavens. Modern medicine uses radiotherapy techniques to detect cancer, blood clots, and other fatal diseases. Cobalt-60 treats cancer tumors and Iodine-131 is used in the treatment of many diseases. Research on antimatter may hold the key for cheap and efficient, low-waste energy production in the future. The HILAC and cyclotrons today are capable of accelerating elements as heavy as uranium to atom smashing speeds, thus opening a pathway for heavier elements not yet discovered. The impact of these few machines has been felt internationally. From a naming scandal to a voyager space probe powered by a plutonium reactor exploring the galaxy. The LINAC will continue to advance the research for the betterment of mankind and pave the future for a more efficient use of the Earth's resources.

Cited Works

1. Wikipedia, The online encyclopedia. <http://en.wikipedia.org/wiki/Uranium> (April 1, 2006).

2. *Nobel Lectures, Physics 1901-1921*, Elsevier Publishing Company, Amsterdam, 1967.

3. Wikipedia, The online encyclopedia. <http://en.wikipedia.org/wiki/Neutron> (April 1, 2006).

4. Hoffman, Darlene C; Ghiorso, Albert; Seaborg, Glenn T. *Transuranium People;* Imperial College Press World Scientific: River Edge, N.J., 2000; pp 10-26.

5. Wikipedia, The online encyclopedia. <http://en.wikipedia.org/wiki/Linear_accelerator> (17 March, 2006).

6. Journal of Chemical Education. <http://jchemed.chem.wisc.edu/JCEWWW/Features/eChemists/Bios/Harris.html> (April 2, 2006).

7. Sullivan, W. *New York Times*, April 28, 1969, p 32.

8. Spectrum Chemical facts sheet. <http://www.speclab.com/elements/104.htm> (2006).

9. *CRC Handbook of Chemistry and Physics*. 84th Edition 2003-2004;

Lide, David R., Ed.;. CRC Press: 2003.

10. Radiochemistry Society. <http://www.radiochemistry.org/ periodictable/elements/104.html> (April 1, 2006).

11. Radiochemistry Society. <http://www.radiochemistry.org/ periodictable/elements/105.html> (April 1, 2006).

12. Hoffman, Darlene C; Ghiorso, Albert; Seaborg, Glenn T. *Transuranium People;* Imperial College Press World Scientific: River Edge, N.J., 2000; pp 387-389.

13. Hoffman, Darlene C; Ghiorso, Albert; Seaborg, Glenn T. *Transuranium People;* Imperial College Press World Scientific: River Edge, N.J., 2000; pp 379-387

14. Wikipedia.com, the online encyclopedia. <http://en.wikipedia. org/wiki/Element_naming_ controversy> (March 31, 2006).

15. Wikipedia.com, the online encyclopedia. <http://en.wikipedia. org/wiki/Thermonuclear_fusion > (April 3, 2006).

16. "Modern Marvels: Nuclear Technology". History Channel. (April 1, 2006.)

17. Live from CERN. <http://livefromcern. web.cern.ch/livefromcern/antimatter> (April 3, 2006).

Images from: www.webelements.com, http://en.wikipedia.org/wiki/Image: Fermilab.jpg, http://en.wikipedia. org/wiki/SLAC, http://www. atomicarchive.com/Fission/Images/ fission.jpg, http://www.sfa-fuzija. si/images/fusion.jpg, http://www. scienzagiovane.unibo.it/English/ antimatter/images/idrogeno-anti. gif, http://livefromcern.web.cern. ch/livefromcern/antimatter/kids/ AM-kids02.html

Chemical & Engineering News January 12, 1998 Copyright © 1998 by the American Chemical Society
Periodic table's size and shape have changed since 1923

Nearly one-fourth (23%) of all the known elements (those in color) have been added to the periodic table since 1923, including all 20 that have atomic numbers greater than that of uranium, element 92. Most of the new elements (those in red) were first created synthetically through nuclear reactions, although several of these elements were later found to be naturally occurring as well. A new row, representing the actinide series, was added to the periodic table in 1945. Elements in color with atomic numbers smaller than that of uranium were assumed to exist but were undiscovered in 1923; those in blue were discovered by isolation from natural sources.

Figure 1. Periodic Table of Elements

Figure 2. Uranium in glass.

Figure 3. Cyclotron.

Figure 4. Linear particle accelerator at Stanford University.

Figure 5. James Andrew Harris,
Huston-Tillotson Alumnus and member of
Ghiorso Research Team Courtesy of HT Public Relations

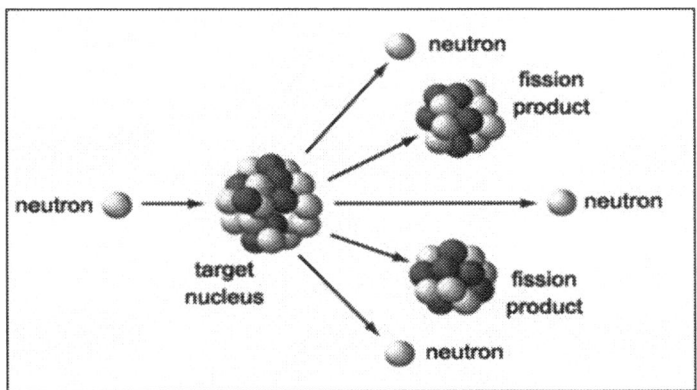

Figure 6. Nuclear fission.

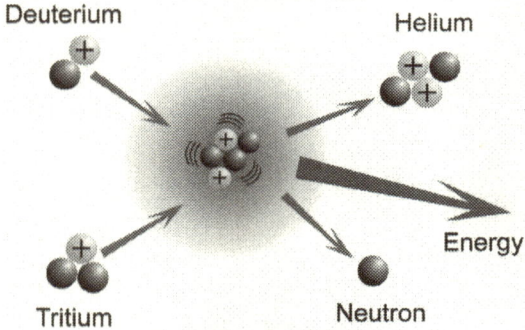

Figure 7. Nuclear fusion.

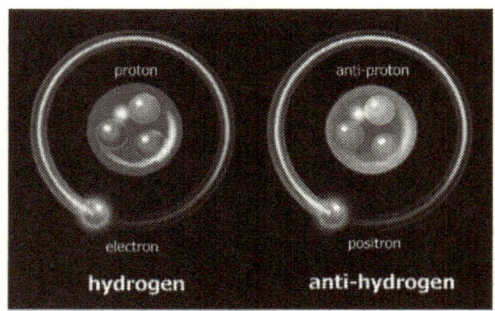

Figure 8. Antimatter: opposite particles.

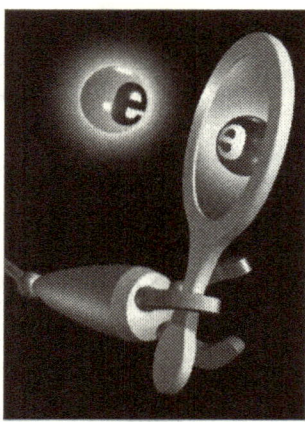

Figure 9. Antimatter a reflection of matter.

Changing the Future:
A Review of the Contributions of
Drs. Kenneth and Mamie Clark

Lynn M. Speed
Junior, Psychology Major

Dr. Debra L Murphy, Major Advisor for Psychology

Kenneth and Mamie Clark met at Howard University, not knowing that they would change the future of education. Dr. Mamie Clark's master's thesis research revealed that segregation in the South affected the self concepts of minority children by instilling emotional anxieties about the color of their skin. In her famous doll study, the children's preferences for the white doll implied that white was the right or proper color to be. It displayed the obvious notion that segregation caused African American children to feel inferior and have maladaptive attitudes. This research is significantly important because it was an effective entity in the groundbreaking case of Brown versus the Board of Education, which brought a legal end to segregation and thereby changed the entire world. Further milestones included this being the first instance of the use of social science research in a Supreme Court case. The "Drs. Clark" served to inspire the next generation of African American researchers to extend their research to give insight into the emotional issues that African American children may be dealing with in the diverse public school system of today.

Keywords: self esteem; Brown versus Board of Education; social action research; African Americans

Introduction

The mind of a child is very fragile. One can only imagine how much of a distorted view can be internalized among children when they are constantly being put down or criticized in school and outside of school. African American children, as well as, adults in the 1930's and 1940's knew all too well about inferiority and low self-esteem. One could only dream of what a child going through segregation would feel about themselves and the way others perceive them. It would be pretty difficult for a parent to tell their child to be proud and love themselves when there is a constant struggle for acceptance and approval in a society that is divided.

Drs. Kenneth and Mamie Clark scientifically researched and tested the mental and emotional impact of these indignities on African American children. The researchers created a milestone with their investigation of how segregation affected the self-concept of African-American children.

Their research on how segregation affected African American children's attitude toward Black and White dolls was a direct reflection of the attitudes that society was instilling in all African American children at that time. African American people were viewed and treated negatively in comparison to Whites. This gave African American children the impression that they were not as good as their counterparts, leaving their self-esteem inadequate compared to White children. This was reflected in the Clark and Clark doll experiment which was the essential evidence that led to the passing of the Brown v. Board of Education legislation. The experiments gave obvious explanation to the effects of segregation in schools. The children perceived themselves as being intellectually inferior because of the forced separation from their White peers in the learning environment. This research gave legislators the evidence that segregation was detrimental to the psychological development of African American children. For the first time in American history, psychological research, including social science evidentiary work of any kind, was used as critical support in possibly the most important court decision in the 20th century (Philogene, 2003).

The Clarks combined their scholarship with activism and authorship at a time when these kinds of accomplishments by African-Americans or other racial/ethnic minority groups were very rarely highlighted. They could not have imagined the extent of their impact on the future of African-Americans' culture and education, the United States, and the entire world. They were fundamentally changed as a result of desegregation (Philogene, 2003).

Literature Review

Kenneth and Mamie Clark met at Howard University, and they became extremely influential psychologists in the field of research. Their work illuminated the understanding about social issues that relate to the self-esteem and self-concepts of African-Americans today (Jones, 2004).

Kenneth Clark was born in the Panama Canal in 1914. Against his father's wishes, Kenneth's mother moved the family to Harlem, New York, where he started attending public schools. Kenneth went to school with a mixture of cultures, but was encouraged to go to a vocational school for a high school education. Kenneth's mother advised him that his education would take him anywhere he wanted to go in the world, and he chose to go to a school for arts and science. Kenneth eventually changed his studies from economics and biology, to the psychology of racism (Columbia University Libraries, 2006).

Mamie Phipps was born in Hot Springs, Arkansas in 1917. She had first hand experience in segregated education while in her primary years. Her father was the only African American physician in the town, so the amount of respect in this small segregated city for his family was better than the normal treatment of African Americans, but she recognized how race played such an important part of society outside of her family (Columbia University Libraries, 2006).

After high school graduation, Kenneth went to Howard University, where he led demonstrations against segregation in Washington, D.C. Mamie entered Howard in 1934 where she intended to study math. She and Kenneth met and immediately connected. Together they broadened each other's perspectives and soon Mamie switched her study to psychology. They focused on the role that race played in their own development, as well as, other

African-American children (Columbia University Libraries, 2006).

Her senior year they got married and moved to New York. Kenneth received his bachelor's and master's degrees from Howard and was the first African American to earn a doctorate in psychology from Columbia University. He taught psychology at Howard and Hampton Institute and published a number of works. After marriage, Kenneth and Mamie Clark both began involvement in civil rights activism. She graduated *magna cum laude* from Howard University and interned that summer with a young lawyer, William Houston. He was instrumental in the early planning of challenging segregationist laws and schooled Mamie in the psychological effects of segregation in the South (Columbia University Libraries, 2006).

Her master's thesis, *The Development of Consciousness of Self in Negro Pre-School Children*, came from her work with African American children in segregated public nursery schools, where she conducted psychology tests using dolls. Research has shown that children become aware of their racial identity—and of society's negative view of blackness—at about 3 years old (Jones, R.L., 2004). She gave the children crayons with pictures of children, and asked them to color the children according to how they saw themselves. Her findings revealed that the children had emotional anxieties in terms of the colors of their own skin. With further experimentation, African American children were given the choice of an African American or white doll to play with, and over half preferred the white doll (Columbia University Libraries, 2006). Mamie's continual studies led to the idea that African American children didn't accept

being Black as the "right" thing to be, leaving them feeling that they were inferior to Whites. It was concluded that African American children had received negative images from their environment that influenced them to develop maladaptive attitudes. The Clarks dealt with negative racial attitudes and opinions on a daily basis, while pursuing their dissertations and even in the workplace. It was the fuel that was used to lay down the framework for how societal influences can influence one's self esteem and self-concept (Columbia University Libraries, 2006). She and Kenneth developed these studies further in a fellowship proposal that enabled Mamie to continue her work at Columbia University. In 1943, she became the first African American woman to earn a Ph.D. in psychology from Columbia University (Philogene, 2003).

Meanwhile, Kenneth had become colleagues and friends with lawyers at the NAACP who were involved in getting schools desegregated. The lawyers needed research on evidence about the mental and emotional effect that segregation had on children. Clark's research demonstrated segregation's impact on African American children's feelings of inferiority and academic performance. Many African American children at the time (1939-1950) "indicated a preference for white and some of them evidenced emotional conflict (bizarre responses) when requested to indicate a color preference." Clark went on to write, "It is clear that the Negro child, by the age of five is aware of the fact that to be colored in contemporary American society is a mark of inferior status" (Clark, 1950). Thurgood Marshall, felt that the Clark's research would be an effective entity in the Brown v. Board of Education case in

1950 (Columbia University Libraries, 2006).

In the court's unanimous decision, as written by Chief Justice Earl Warren: "Segregation of white and colored children in public schools has a detrimental effect upon the colored children. The impact is greater when it has the sanction of law; for the policy of separating the races is usually interpreted as denoting the inferiority of the Negro group. A sense of inferiority affects the motivation of a child to learn. Segregation with the sanction of law, therefore, has the tendency to retard the educational and mental development of Negro children and to deprive them of some of the benefits they would receive in a racially integrated school system"(American Psychological Association, 2006). Segregation did not provide African American and White children equal protection under the law, as should have been guaranteed by the 14th amendment. Segregation was unconstitutional, and "what started out as a minor research project became a very important historical footnote" (American Psychological Association, 2006).

Figure 1 Dolls

Figure 2 The "Drs. Clark"

Though that is what the Clarks are famous for, their other areas of research also had a significant impact on African Americans and the larger society, as well. This other additional "social action" type research has served as a model for the current generation of African-American psychologists, including the author, who has always desired working with children to facilitate their interaction with psychologists to improve their academic performance and mental and social health.

Mamie Clark's Northside Center for Child Development in 1946 exemplifies this type of research. She founded the first center to provide therapy for children in Harlem. The Northside Center for Development was established for children that are emotionally disturbed. The center was to provide psychiatric therapy, psychological diagnosis and counseling, psychiatric social work for parents and children, and other kinds of additional services, such as remedial reading, medical diagnosis, and multicultural recreation for children. Public schools were illegally forcing enrollment of many African American children into programs for the mentally handicapped. However, the center conducted its own intelligence tests, opposed the schools, and empowered the community. Realizing that therapy could not by itself address the detrimental affects of racism, Northside also assisted families with their housing and economic difficulties (Northside Center for Child Development, 2006).

Mamie and Kenneth hoped that their center would help to get rid of the negative perceptions of African American people. Kenneth and Mamie felt as though the psychoanalysis of Freud was standard for middle class white children, but not culturally appropriate for African American children in Harlem, although the Board was insistent upon this focus (Philogene, 2003). In addition to the Northside Center, in June 1962, Kenneth Clark established Harlem Youth Opportunities Unlimited (HARYOU) to reorganize the schools of Harlem by integrating classes, enforcing higher standards on teachers, and involving parents and other community members in the education of its young people. It was to be the trial product for the type of community action programs that would come into play in the 1980s and 1990s. His dream would never materialize. The federal government in May 1964 allocated $110 million for the program, and arranged a merger of HARYOU with Associated Community Teams (ACT), a group which Democratic Congressman Adam Clayton Powell ultimately supported. Clark and Powell disagreed over the program's leadership and Clark resigned from the organization on July 31, 1964 (Columbia University Libraries, 2006).

The contributions of Kenneth and Mamie Clark have spanned the spectrum, including education, literature, and politics. Kenneth

became the first African American permanent professor at City College of New York, where he remained until his retirement in 1975. Additionally, he was the first African American to join the New York Board of Regents and to serve as president of the American Psychological Association. He also published a number of books and articles. His most famous was "Dark Ghetto: *Dilemmas of Social Power*" *(1965)*. Mamie served on the boards of organizations such as the American Broadcast Company, Mount Sinai Medical Center, the Museum of Modern Art, and the New York Public Library.

Discussion

The Clark and Clark Doll Study was the first time that social science research was used in a Supreme Court case. Not only is that African-American history, but it is dually noted in psychology, sociology, philosophy, and law chronicles. These researchers put together evidence to show how at one point, this country was responsible for education that detrimentally affected the psychological development of young African Americans. Their research has contributed to a better understanding of how social forces, such as racism, impact the development of African-Americans' self-esteem, self-concept, and cultural pride. This research has given the author and other aspiring African American psychologists insight into the emotional issues that African American children in the past dealt with and may still be dealing with in the diverse, but still defacto segregated, public school system of today. This author has hopes of impacting society to better African American people through research on understanding the effect of societal factors on the educational and social advancement and psychological health of African Americans.

The findings of predecessors, such as the "Drs. Clark" have served to inspire others to pursue a career in research. Kenneth and Mamie Clark's persistence and commitment allowed fellow African Americans of this generation to understand the concept and benefits of being inferior to no one and not allowing other people's views and opinions to cloud the just of one's true self. This research has not only changed the lives of the African American community, but American society as a whole. Social science research is critical to the entire spectrum of youth development and their education. It has made a mark in public policy, the judicial system, and psychological advancement, of course. The research of these educators behooved the author and other young aspiring psychologist to engage in social action type service and research that will help the African American community and culture when it comes to children and their success. Hopefully, future research of this type will have as much of an impact on this culture as did the monumental work of the Clarks.

References

Clark, Kenneth B. & Clark, Mamie K. The development of consciousness of self and the emergence of racial identification in Negro preschool children. *Journal of Social Psychology, S.P.S.S.I. Bulletin.* 1939; *10*, 591-599.

Clark, Kenneth B. & Clark, Mamie K. (1940). Skin color as a factor in racial identification of Negro preschool children. *Journal of Social Psychology, S.P.S.S.I. Bulletin, 11*. 1940; 159-169.

Clark, K. B. & Clark, M. K. Emotional factors in racial identification and preference in Negro children. *Journal of Negro Education, 19*. 1950; 341-350.

Jones, Reginald L. *Black Psychology, Fourth Edition.*, Virginia, Cobb and Henry Publishers, 2004

Philogene, Gina. *Racial Identity in Context: The Legacy of Kenneth B. Clark.*, Washington, D.C., American Psychology Association, 2004.

http://www.findarticles.com/

Northside Center for Child Development. Retrieved 7,7, 2006 http://www.northsidecenter.org/new/default.htm

Columbia University Libraries Oral History Research Office. Retrieved July, 7, 2006. http://www.columbia.edu/cu/lweb/digital/collections/nny/index.html

American Psychology Association. Retrieved July, 7, 2006. http://www.psychologymatters.org/clark.html

JFlo at the movies. Retrieved Feb., 13, 2007. http://blog.courttv.com/jami_floyd/at_the_movies/index.html

Images from: http://blog.courttv.com/jami_floyd/at_the_movies/index.html,

II. Current Research at Huston-Tillotson University

Initial Internal Control Assessments
Under Section 404 of SOX

Willie Howard
Senior, Business Administration
Jennifer De Loach
Senior, Business Administration

Louis Perez
Junior, Business Administration
Douglas Lumpkin
Junior, Accounting

Dr. Robert Kellogg, Major Advisor for Business Administration

The most controversial requirements of Sarbanes-Oxley (SOX) are the mandated management evaluations of internal controls. The first internal control assessments were included in 10-K reports filed with the SEC in early 2005 and provide new information about the state of financial reporting processes in corporate America. A random sample of these filings is analyzed to develop a meaningful classification of control deficiencies and to test causes and effects of variations in internal control quality. Results raise questions about the SOX implementation scheme that bases control effectiveness on a "material weakness" concept borrowed from auditing standards.

Key Words: Sarbanes-Oxley, Section 404, Internal Control

Data are available from public sources.

Introduction

The importance of internal control over financial reporting has long been recognized (see Kinney et al. 1990), but the Sarbanes-Oxley Act of 2002 has elevated interest to an unprecedented level. Law commentators have called the internal control provisions of SOX (section 404) and the SEC rules implementing them "a fundamental change in the securities laws, one that elevates procedure to almost the same prominence as substance." (Huber & Hoffman 2004) The SEC's adopting release (SEC 2003) required accelerated filers to provide internal control assessments for fiscal years ending on or after June 15, 2004, but in February 2004, as corporations protested the costs created by the rules (Solomon & Bryan-Low 2004), the compliance dates were extended until November 15, 2004. (SEC 2004)

SEC Rule 15d-15 requires:

The management of each such issuer ... must evaluate, with the participation of the issuer's principal executive and principal financial officers, or persons performing similar functions, the effectiveness, as of the end of each fiscal year, of the issuer's internal control over financial reporting. The framework on which management's evaluation of the issuer's internal control over financial reporting is based must be a suitable, recognized control framework that is established by a body or group that has followed due-process procedures, including the broad distribution of the framework for public comment.

SEC rules incorporate the concept of "material weakness" that is included in generally accepted auditing and attestation standards promulgated by the AICPA (2001, 2002). Management is precluded from determining that a company's internal control over financial reporting is effective if it identifies one or more material weaknesses in the company's internal control over financial reporting, and management's report must include disclosure of any material weakness identified during the course of its evaluation. (Item 308(d) of Regulations S-B and S-K)

438 accelerated filers were identified that included internal control assessments in annual reports (Form 10-K) filed with the SEC during the first six months of 2005. We analyzed a random sample of 30 of these filings to determine:

a. the number and nature of material weaknesses disclosed,
b. the effects of firm size on internal control effectiveness,
c. the effects of material weaknesses on firms' profitability, and
d. the effects of material weaknesses on firms' market values.

First, the sample is described, and reported material weaknesses are classified using the COSO typolology of internal control components. Next, material weaknesses are examined as conditions associated with firm size. The presence of material weaknesses is then related to accounting measures of firm performance and market returns surrounding announcements of internal control effectiveness. Finally, conclusions are stated that support substantive changes in the section 404 implementation scheme.

Thirty Accelerated Filers and Reported Material Weaknesses

The restricted size of our sample requires an evaluation of how well it represents the population of all accelerated filers of internal control assessments. In addition, although our interest is in the existence or absence of material weaknesses as a bimodal classification, descriptions of specific control deficiencies included in sampled assessments provides content to the classification.

Industry Representation.

It is well-established that corporate reporting is influenced by industry

| | **Table One** | | |
| | **Industry Representation** | | |
Industry Sector	**# in sample**	**% in sample**	**% of filers**
Retail	11	37%	14%
Consumer Products Manufacturers	5	17%	5%
Business Services	4	13%	15%
Electronics	2	7%	11%
Metals & Mining	2	7%	3%
Energy & Utilities	1	3%	4%
Financial Services	1	3%	16%
Health Care	1	3%	3%
Industrial Manufacturing	1	3%	5%
Pharmaceuticals	1	3%	3%
Transportation Services	1	3%	3%
Grand Total	30	100%	82%

effects. (See, e.g. Palmrose et al 2002) The 30 firms studied come from 11 different industry sectors (Table One). Compared with all accelerated filers, two sectors—retail and consumer products—are overrepresented in the sample. More troubling is that sectors including 18% of accelerated filers are not represented in the sample.

Material Weaknesses Reported.

Auditing Standard 2 of the Public Company Accounting Oversight Board (PCAOB 2004) provides the definition of "material weakness" that is incorporated into the SEC internal control assessment requirements. There is a three-stage development of the definition in Auditing Standard No. 2.

First, a **control deficiency** exists "when the design or operation of a control does not allow management or employees, in the normal course of performing their assigned functions, to prevent or detect misstatements on a timely basis." (at paragraph 8)

Second, **a significant deficiency** is "a control deficiency, or combination of control deficiencies, that adversely affects the company's ability to initiate, authorize, record, process, or report external financial data reliably in accordance with generally accepted accounting principles such that there is more than a remote likelihood that a misstatement of the company's annual or interim financial statements that is more than inconsequential will not be prevented or detected." (at paragraph 9)

Finally, a **material weakness** is defined as "a significant deficiency, or combination of significant deficiencies, that results in more than a remote likelihood that a material misstatement of the annual or interim financial statements will not be prevented or detected." (at paragraph 10)

Furthermore, Auditing Standard No. 2 lists specific conditions that have presumed significance. Deficiencies in the following areas constitute "**at least significant deficiencies**" (paragraph 139):

- Controls over the selection and application of accounting policies;
- Antifraud programs and controls;
- Controls over non-routine and non-systematic transactions; and
- Controls over the period-end financial reporting process.

The standard also specifies circumstances that each should be regarded as "**at least a significant deficiency and as a strong indicator that a material weakness exists**" as follows (paragraph 140):

- Restatement of previously issued financial statements to reflect the correction of a misstatement due to error or fraud.
- Identification by the auditor of a material misstatement in financial statements in the current period that was not initially identified by the company's internal control over financial reporting.
- Oversight of the company's external financial reporting and internal control over financial reporting by the company's audit committee is ineffective.
- The internal audit function or the risk assessment function is ineffective at a company in which violations of laws and regulations could have a material effect on the reliability of financial reporting.
- Identification of fraud of any magnitude on the part of senior management.
- Significant deficiencies that have been communicated to management and the audit committee remain uncorrected after some reasonable period of time.
- An ineffective control environment.

In practice, as represented by accelerated filers' Item 9A filings, material weaknesses are identified as either operational deficiencies or errors in specific accounts. Ge and McVay (2005) provide the first analysis of reported material weakness and choose to classify them according to accounts affected. A major rating agency, however, expresses a preference for classification based on COSO criteria. (Doss & Jonas 2004) Consistent with this, the SEC endorses the use of the COSO framework (Committee of Sponsoring Organizations 1992) for evaluating internal controls. (SEC 2003 at II B 3 a) We classify material weaknesses reported by the sampled companies using the five COSO internal control components in Table Two.

Table Two		
Material Weakness by COSO Component		
COSO Component	**# of MWs**	**# of Firms**
Monitoring	23	13
Control Activities	12	5
Control Environment	15	7
Information System	10	5
Risk Assessment	1	1

Seventeen (57%) of the 30 sampled firms reported ineffective controls due to one or more material weaknesses. We were able to classify 61 (an average of 3.6 per firm) of these as representing weakness in a COSO component. Table Two indicates that monitoring deficiencies constitute the most frequent reason given for unfavorable internal control assessments. Further conceptual work is needed to justify inferences and specify testable hypotheses based on this classification. For example, are monitoring and control environment related aspects of an organizational commitment to financial reporting quality? This query conceptualizes control activities and the information system as mere mechanical operations

that implement management's preferred approach to information delivery and suggests approaches to corporate governance issues.

The Effect of Firm Size on Internal Control Over Financial Reporting

Ge and McVay (2005) fail to find an association between firm size and the occurrence of material weaknesses. Although they cite Sarbanes-Oxley (SOX) as motivating their work, their results are based on quarterly reports prior to first filings under section 404 of SOX in early 2005. The researchers indirectly acknowledge this by focusing on "the types of material weakness that investors **might expect to see**" under section 404. (Ge and McVey at 141, emphasis added). We test Ge and McVay's findings using the actual results of 404 evaluations.

Intuitively, firm size may or may not be a determinant of good internal control. While large firms have more assets that must be controlled, large firms also tend to have more employees and greater resources to spend on internal auditors and consulting fees that contribute to internal control effectiveness. (Ashbaugh et al 2005) Researchers like Ge and McVay use market capitalization (MARKET CAP) to measure firm size, and we adopt this measure for two reasons: (1) it is reported in the 10-Ks that contain the section 404 assessments, and (2) it measures a firm's financial capacity and need for reporting controls better than total assets or revenues.

Table Three reports MARKET CAP statistics for firms in the sample.

Both the mean and median firm size are greater for firms reporting no material weaknesses. The T-Statistic for

Table Three					
Descriptive Statistics of Firm Size					
	Market Capitalization ($millions)				
	Mean	Median	Smallest	Largest	Std Dev
All Firms n=30	481.8	426.1	45.2	2400	436.3
Material Weakness n=17	474.9	230.6	45.2	2400	555.5
Effective Controls n=13	490.9	472	252.6	944.4	220.1

the mean difference between the market caps of the two groups, however, is .75 and not significant.

Table Three also highlights the existence of an obvious outlier in the Material Weakness group – Baxter International with a market cap of 2.4 billion dollars, which is nearly five times the sample mean. When Baxter is omitted, the standard deviation of the Material Weakness group is halved, and the T-Statistic of 1.90 is significant at the 10% level (probability of .068). Descriptive statistics with Baxter omitted are reported in Table Four.

The effect of Baxter on test statistics merits additional comment. The Baxter 10-K describes the reported material weakness as follows:

Specifically, current income taxes payable balances were not reconciled to expected tax payments due, and the company did not adequately review the difference between the income tax basis and the financial reporting basis of assets and liabilities, and reconcile the difference to recorded deferred income tax assets and liabilities. (Baxter International 2005)

The significance of this deficiency for the overall effectiveness of the company's internal control is debatable and suggests that conclusions about the causes and consequences of internal control deficiencies will require large-sample analysis of specific material weaknesses.

Table Four					
Descriptive Statistics of Firm Size (Baxter omitted)					
	Market Capitalization ($millions)				
	Mean	Median	Smallest	Largest	Std Dev
All Firms n=30	481.8	426.1	45.2	2400	436.3
Material Weakness n=16	354.6	230.1	45.2	930.3	258.1
Effective Controls n=13	490.9	472	252.6	944.4	220.1

The Effect of Internal Control on Profitability

Although Sarbanes-Oxley and implementation of Section 404 by the SEC give little attention to the effects of internal control on operational efficiency, both professionals and researchers consider such effects important. Doss and Jonas (2005) in a special comment by a prominent assurance agency expect effects on operations to be important to bond ratings. Ge and McVay (2005 at 151) hypothesize that "firm disclosures of material weaknesses are likely to be negatively associated associated with profitability" and use pre-104 filings to test effects on return to assets and cash flow. They find little association with control deficiencies, however.

We used our sample of first filers of Section 404 reports to determine the effects of material weaknesses on firms' Return on Equity (ROE) by comparing reported ROE of the 13 firms with effective internal controls (no material weaknesses) to that of the 17 firms with ineffective controls (material weaknesses reported).

ROE statistics for sampled firms are reported in Table Five.

The contrast between the two groups is pronounced – firms with effective controls experienced positive ROE of 17.2% on average compared with the negative ROE of -9.8% of the material weakness firms. The T-Statistic for the difference is 2.57, significant at less than 2%, suggesting that more powerful tests of internal control effects result from using Section 404 reports to differentiate firms. Ge and McVay's results were based on a comparison of material weakness firms with all other Compustat firms, about which no information on internal control effectiveness was considered.

V. The Impact of Filings and Material Weaknesses on Stock Prices

An SEC commissioner has recognized the importance of research to the continuing implementation of SOX: "Does the fact that a company discloses material weaknesses have any affect on its stock price?" One would expect the market to price a risk premium into a company's stock, depending on the weakness identified. Has that been the case with any of these companies to date? We would encourage economists and investors to take the time to consider these questions." (Atkins 2005)

In order to respond to Commissioner Atkins' query, we analyzed stock

Table Five

ROE of 30 Accelerated Filers

		Return On Equity (%)				
		Mean	Median	Smallest	Largest	Std Dev
All Firms	n=30	1.9	8.26	-147.44	79.92	36.84
Material Weakness	n=17	-9.8	4.52	-147.44	18.85	42.75
Effective Controls	n=13	17.2	11.79	3.6	79.92	19.89

prices of the sampled firms. To date, no published research has provided evidence on the issue. Working papers have reported mixed results for market reactions to disclosures of material weaknesses. Hammersley et al. (2005) document a negative market reaction for firms reporting material weaknesses in 302 disclosures and De Franco et al. (2005) also find negative abnormal returns for firms that report internal control problems. However, Emanuels et al. (2005) find significantly negative market reactions in the period prior to the disclosure event, but not at the disclosure. Ashbough et al. (2005), Bryan and Lilien (2005) and Li et al (2006) find no negative market reactions to material weakness disclosures.

None of these studies compare returns to firms disclosing material weaknesses with those to firms reporting effective controls with no material weaknesses. When we do this, we find negative returns subsequent to disclosures of material weaknesses.

Observed Returns Conditioned by Section 404 Disclosures

Returns to common shareholders are derived using stock prices before and after Section 404 internal control evaluations are filed with the SEC. Average returns during an 11 day window surrounding Form 10-K filings containing firms' first Section 404 assessments are reported in Table Six. Returns to an equally-weighted portfolio of 13 firms that reported no weaknesses are compared to returns to an equally-weighted portfolio of 17 firms that reported material weaknesses.

The greatest daily difference in returns occurs on the day after internal control disclosure (Day 1) shares of firms with no material weaknesses recording a daily return on average 2.6% greater than the average return to shares of firms with material weaknesses. The only statistically significant difference in returns, however, occurs on the day before disclosure (Day -1) when the shares of firms with material weaknesses perform better on average than other firms.

Average daily returns are charted in Graph One, and the pronounced differences related to the content of internal disclosures on days -1 and 1 are striking.

Cumulative returns during the 11 days surrounding 10-K filings are reported in Table Seven. On average,

Table Six										
Average Daily Returns (%) Surrounding Internal Control Disclosures										
Day	-5	-4	-3	-2	-1	Filing	1	2	3	4	5
All Firms (n=30)	0.35	0.05	0.22	0.27	0.74	0.77	-0.27	0.28	0.00	-0.25	-0.52
No MW (n=13)	-0.18	-0.22	-0.08	0.75	0.15	0.46	1.22	-0.51	0.14	0.15	-0.34
MW (n=17)	0.76	0.26	0.45	-0.09	1.43	1.01	-1.41	0.87	-0.11	-0.56	-0.65
t	1.54	0.57	0.67	1.20	2.02	0.52	1.05	0.84	0.35	1.38	0.20
Probability	0.14	0.58	0.51	0.24	0.05	0.60	0.30	0.41	0.73	0.18	0.84

27

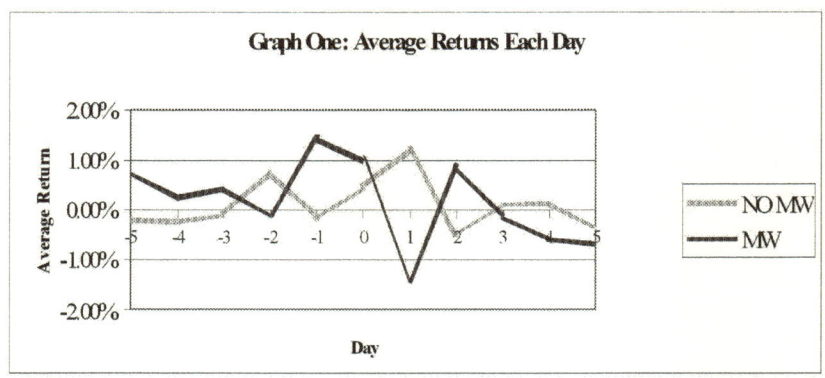

firms reporting material weaknesses fare better, gaining 1.85% to 1.32% for other firms. The cumulative returns are shown in Graph Two.

Returns figures and the graph indicate that the comparative gains to shareholders of the firms with material weaknesses peak (3.9% to .58%) on the filing date and erode over the subsequent five days. In fact, once the existence of material weaknesses is disclosed, a firm, on average, provides negative five-day returns (-1.9%) to its shareholders. In contrast, shareholders of firms that disclose effective internal controls receive positive five-day returns (.5%). The final graph portrays the divergent return experience subsequent to disclosure.

Table Seven										
Cumulative Returns (%) From Five Days Before Internal Control Disclosures										
Day	-5	-4	-3	-2	-1	Filing	1	2	3	4	5
No MW (n=13)	-0.18	-0.41	-0.49	0.25	0.08	0.58	2.11	1.60	1.57	1.68	1.32
MW (n=17)	0.76	1.01	1.48	1.36	2.83	3.90	2.36	3.24	3.11	2.53	1.85
t	1.61	1.60	1.46	0.80	1.71	1.50	0.07	0.41	0.44	0.25	0.15
Prob	0.12	0.12	0.16	0.43	0.10	0.14	0.95	0.69	0.67	0.81	0.88

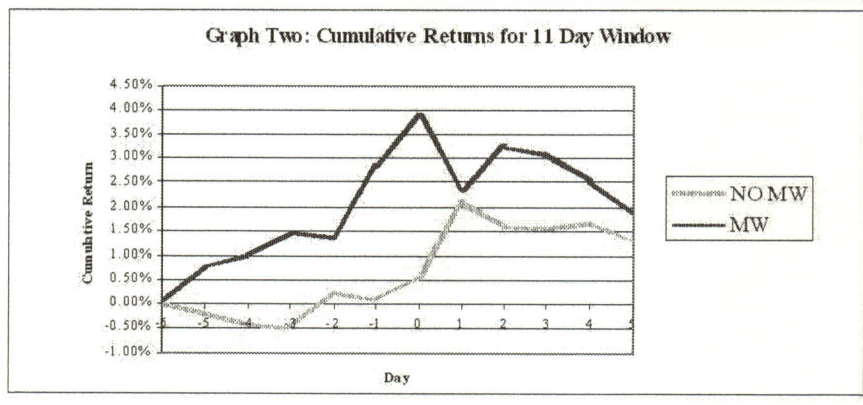

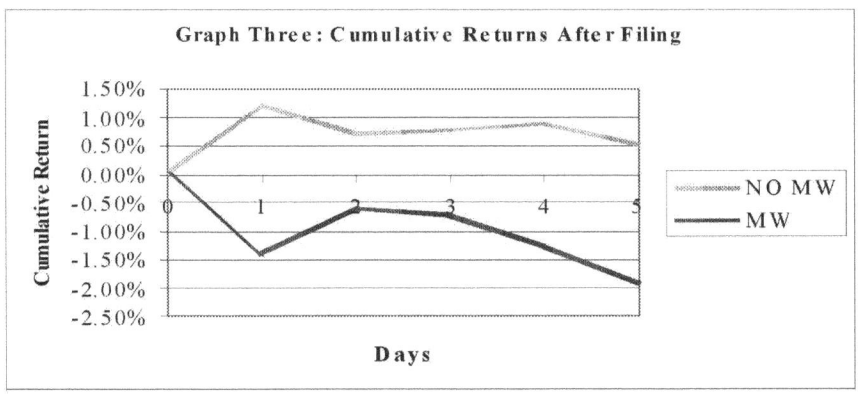

Conclusions

As reported in first Section 404 evaluations, monitoring deficiencies constitute the most frequent reason given for unfavorable internal control assessments. Further research is needed to develop and test expectations regarding the effects of different material weakness types, but it is reasonable to note that the SOX "weakness-no weakness" reporting rules allow no gradations in reported internal control effectiveness.

Some evidence is presented that firm size is associated with effective internal controls. The small sample allows a single outlier to have a dramatic effect on test statistics. Close examination of the anomaly suggests that the firm size-internal control relationship is likely to depend on specific characteristics of control deficiencies. Again we suggest that future development of SOX implementation consider internal control assessments based on a refined material weakness classification.

Firms reporting material weaknesses exhibit lower accounting returns to equity than firms with effective internal controls. There is some evidence that this translates into relatively poor stock returns: subsequent to disclosure, firms with material weaknesses experience negative returns. In contrast, shareholders of firms that disclose effective internal controls receive positive five-day returns. Previous failures to find a market reaction to disclosure of material weaknesses may result from not comparing returns of firms asserting different levels of internal control effectiveness.

References

AICPA 2001. "Reporting on an Entity's Internal Control Over Financial Reporting," (Codified as AT §501) New York.

_____ 2002. "Communication of Internal Control Related Matters Noted in an Audit,"(Codified as AU §325) New York.

Ashbaugh, H., D. Collins, and W. Kinney. 2005. "The discovery and consequences of internal control deficiencies prior to SOX-mandated audits," Working Paper, University of Wisconsin-Madison.

Atkins, P. 2005. "Speech by SEC Commissioner: Remarks before the Joint Meeting of SEC Government-Business Forum on Small Business Capital Formation Forum and the SEC Advisory Committee on Smaller Public Companies, September 19, 2005."

Baxter International. 2005. "Annual Report on Form 10-K, March 2005."

Bryan, S. and S. Lilien. 2005. "Characteristics of firms with material weaknesses in internal control: an assessment of Section 404 of Sarbanes-Oxley," Working Paper, Wake Forest University.

Committee of Sponsoring Organizations 1992. "Internal Control: Integrated Framework," New York.

De Franco G.D.; Y Guan and H Lu. 2005. "The wealth change and redistribution effects of Sarbanes-Oxley internal control disclosures" Working Paper, University of Toronto.

Doss, Michael and G. Jonas. 2005. "Section 404 Reports on Internal Control: Impact on Ratings Will Depend on Nature of Material Weaknesses Reported," Moody's Special Comment. New York.

Emanuels, J., O. Leeuwen, B. Praag, and P. Wallage. 2005. "Abnormal returns around disclosure of problems in 'internal control over financial reporting'," Working Paper, University of Amsterdam.

Ge, W. and S. McVay. 2005. "The Disclosure of Material Weaknesses in Internal Control after the Sarbanes Oxley Act," *Accounting Horizons* 19, 137-158.

Hammersley, J.S., L. Myers, and C. Shakespeare. 2005. "Market reactions to the disclosure of internal control weaknesses and to the characteristics of those weaknesses under Section 302 of the Sarbanes Oxley Act of 2002,"

Working Paper, University of Georgia.

Huber, J. and J. Hoffman. 2004. "The Sarbanes–Oxley Act of 2002 and SEC Rulemaking," at http://www.lw.com/upload/docs/doc84.pdf.

Kinney, W., M. Maher, and D. Wright. 1990. "Assertions-based standards for integrated internal control" *Accounting Horizons* 4, 1-8.

Li, Chan, S. Scholz, and Q. Wang. 2006. "Internal Control over Financial Reporting: Is the Market Indifferent?" Working Paper, University of Kansas.

Palmrose, Z-V., V. Richardson, and S. Scholz. 2002. "Determinants of Market Reactions to Restatements Announcements," Working Paper, University of Southern California and University of Kansas.

PCAOB 2004. "Auditing Standard No. 2: An Audit of Internal Control Over Financial Reporting Performed in Conjunction With an Audit of Financial Statements," Washington, D.C.

SEC 2003. "Managements's Report on Internal Control Over Financial Reporting and Certification of Disclosure in Exchange Act Periodic Reports. Release No. 33-8238," Washington, D.C.

2004. "Extension of Compliance Dates Regarding Internal Control Over Financial Reporting Requirements. Release No. 33-8392," Washington, D.C.

Solomon, D. and C. Bryan-Low. 2004. "Companies Complain About Cost of Corporate-Governance Rules," *Wall Street Journal*, Feb. 10, 2004, at A1

Cultural Biases: Disparities in Mental Health within the Hispanic Population

Toby J Green
Senior, Psychology

Dr. Debra L Murphy, Major Advisor for Psychology

Hispanics, the largest minority group in the United States, suffer from many disparities in the area of mental health. Factors such as discrimination, racism, social inequality, and cultural barriers perpetuate this disparity. Additionally, ineffective assessment and diagnostic methods continue to plague the mental health field. The focus of this research is to expose cultural insensitivities in the design of the Mood Disorder Questionnaire (MDQ). This tool, used primarily to identify manic traits of bipolar disorder, is a self report questionnaire commonly administered to patients in a clinical setting. Through deep analysis of the semantic design of the MDQ, questions regarding its effectiveness for the Hispanic patient are presented. Research for this study involved direct interviews of Hispanic participants who have agreed to complete the MDQ, and provide specific interpretations of each question. The participants were selected based on ethnicity, English speaking ability, and a reported mental health history. The findings of this project were consistent with the hypothesized conclusion. The data collected presented false positives in all cases. It was concluded that the Mood Disorder Questionnaire is not culturally relevant to the Hispanic patient, and could lead to a gross misdiagnosis which may result in inappropriate treatment.

Keywords: Hispanics; bipolar; Mood Disorder Questionnaire; culture; minority

Introduction

As the Hispanic population increases in the United States, the increased need for competent mental health care services is ever increasing. Cultural barriers that would preclude the delivery of these services are now more than ever impacting this population. Through the deep analysis of one particular psychological assessment tool, this paper seeks to expose external cultural attitudes that may perpetuate this disparity.

The assessment tool, entitled "Mood Disorder Questionnaire" (MDQ) is a series of questions, in English, that seek to identify specific manic traits associated with bipolar disorder, that was developed by Hirschfeld, Spitzer, Calabrese, Flynn, Keck, Lewis, McElroy, Post, Rapport, Russell, Sachs, and Zajecka (2003). The patient is given the survey which asks a variety of questions about personal feelings, general mood, and certain activities. The patient chooses "yes" or "no" for each question by circling their response. Upon completion, the assessment is reviewed and used as a first line determinant for initial diagnosis. Developers of the MDQ,

31

through demographic validation, have concluded that this assessment tool is practical for the screening of Bipolar I and II (Hirschfeld, et al., 2003).

It will be shown, in the forthcoming research, that the percentage of subjects of Hispanic origin was not representative of the population in the United States (U.S. Census Bureau, 2003). At first glance, one can conclude that the assessment was developed with the English-speaking Caucasian patient in mind. It will be the goal of this paper to analyze the chosen phonology and cultural meaning of each question from a Hispanic point of view. At this point it must be pointed out that the term "Hispanic" will be used throughout the paper. It should not be implied that the use of this term carries any association to country of origin, but rather general ethnic background.

Literature Review

In an effort to discover the link between disparities in mental health and cultural attitudes affecting Hispanics in the United States, a review of major scientific studies and research articles must be reviewed. To establish a baseline of mental health distress among Hispanics, a review of the Surgeon General's report on mental health reported specific disparities affecting minorities in the U.S. It reported that minorities have reduced access to and availability of mental health services. Second, minorities have a reduced chance of receiving those services. Third, minority mental health care is of substandard quality. Last, there exists a gross misrepresentation in minority mental health research (DHHS, 1999). Through the DHHS Report, U.S. Surgeon General Satcher sought to communicate a need for change in the delivery of mental health care services to minorities. A direct correlation between cultural attitudes and the quality and effectiveness of the mental health service is made in the article. It remains incumbent upon the mental health provider and delivery system to ensure that services are designed with the recipient in mind. Care must be taken to provide services that meet the needs of racial and ethnic minorities (DHHS, 1999).

Recognized as the largest minority group in the U.S., Hispanic Americans are also the poorest (DHHS, 1999). Some of the socioeconomic (SES) factors that impact Hispanics include language barriers, education, ethnic discrimination, and in some cases a lack of citizenship. It has been shown that these factors have led to increased external locus of control in many Hispanic populations (Mirowsky & Ross, 1984). The idea that one has no control of life's occurrences has been linked to increased psychological distress. In addition to stress, lower SES Hispanics are more likely to report increased depression and hostility (Kouyoumdjian & Hansen, 2003). To further compound the problem, Hispanics must deal with many other stressors that act as barriers to effective mental health care. The article reports "under utilization of mental health services, perceptions of mental illnesses, fatalism, spirituality, and familial and cultural commitment..." (Kouyoumdjian, et al., 2003). The study suggests that a multi-faceted approach is needed to combat these problems, which should include education for patients and providers, cultural sensitivity training, and strategies to reduce the language barrier.

Acculturation and its related stressors also seem to be a factor in the prevalence of mental health disparities among Hispanics. Acculturation is a process by which one culture is affected by another. Acculturative stress can result when a culture strives to preserve its identity. Acculturation has been linked to an increase in psychiatric disorders in Mexican Americans as compared to Mexicans living in Mexico (Burnam, Hough, Karno, Escobar & Telles, 1987). To address this concern, efforts are needed to incorporate elements of the Hispanic culture in the design and implementation of mental health services. Specific measures are needed to deal with stress resulting from acculturation. Specifically DHHS outlines key areas to focus on.. They include identifying service needs, ensuring the availability of services, enabling access to services, promoting the use of services, and evaluating the appropriateness and outcome of the services (DHHS, 1999). To accomplish these goals in the Hispanic population, cultural considerations must be addressed to overcome barriers in service delivery.

An understanding of Hispanic culture or "cultura" is key in order to begin addressing problems in the mental healthcare system. Not only do Hispanics possess different beliefs and views than other Americans, many do not speak English, or they choose Spanish as their primary language. This barrier is unique as it prevents the dissemination of information about services, and is problematic in communicating with non-Spanish speaking providers. Research has been conducted to test the applicability of a bilingual/bicultural psychiatric program. The idea was to deliver mental health care to Hispanics via Hispanic providers. Additionally, all sessions were conducted in Spanish, and considerations were made to include the use of spiritualism, a

significant component of the Hispanic culture. The results were astonishing. Patients were more relaxed and receptive to the treatments. This culturally sensitive program did not require drastic changes in the psychiatric approach, but rather the incorporation of familiar aspects while providing effective care (Santiago-Irizzary, 1996).

Before programs like the above can be implemented, the tools used to initially screen for psychological and psychiatric disorders must be assessed for cultural appropriateness. The MDQ is a screening tool that is a simple, self-report assessment utilized by mental health workers to identify patients with bipolar disorder (Hirschfeld, et al., 2000).

Since the development and implementation of the MDQ, additional validation and research have been conducted to test its effectiveness. In 2003, a study was conducted involving just over 700 adult participants who completed the MDQ. The research group of Hirschfeld, et al., (2003) claimed this study was a "nationwide epidemiological general population sample that was balanced for key demographic variables." However, only 2.3% of the population sample surveyed was Hispanic (Hirschfeld, et al., 2003) while the U.S. Census Bureau (2003) reported that Hispanics comprised 13.9% of the total population in 2003, which suggests that the sample was not representative. More importantly, the total number of Hispanics that participated in the validation equaled approximately 15 persons, which calls into question the psychometric validity of this tool. In Figure 1, the comparison between the U.S. population and the demographic composition of participants used in the MDQ validation is outlined.

33

Figure 1

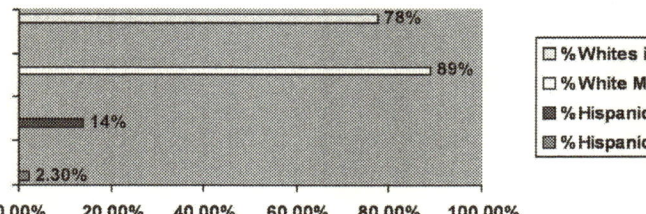

These data show an overrepresentation for the Whites in the population sample by 11 percentage points. and an under representation of the Hispanic population by 11.7 percentage points.

Method

Qualitative methods using deep analysis of the semantic design of the MDQ questions and their interpretation by Hispanic clients were conducted to ascertain their effectiveness for this population. Each question was analyzed in the attempt to identify cultural biases in its design. Hispanic participants were interviewed who agreed to complete the MDQ, and provide specific interpretations of each question.

The extent to which possible cultural differences in interpretation (or misinterpretation) of the questions by Hispanics (predictor variable) may be associated with the resulting diagnosis (or misdiagnosis) was examined. The outcome variable in this case was the diagnosis or misdiagnosis.

The participants were selected based on ethnicity, English speaking ability, and a reported mental health history. Two participants were selected randomly, to answer the questions on the MDQ. The criteria chosen for the participants were:

- Proficient English speaking and reading ability.
- Hispanic ethnicity.

- No previous or current diagnosis of Bipolar I disorder.

The data for this study were collected through the recording of personal interpretations of the MDQ questions by the participants (predictor variable). The responses were recorded as provided by the respondents. Below is the MDQ developed in November 2000, and first published in the American Journal of Psychiatry (Hirschfeld, et al., 2000).

1. Has there ever been a period of time when you were not your usual self and (while not on drugs or alcohol)...

...you felt so good or so hyper that other people thought you were not your normal self or you were so hyper that you got into trouble?

...you were so irritable that you shouted at people or started fights or arguments?

...you felt much more self-confident than usual?

...you got much less sleep than usual and found you didn't really miss it?

...you were much more talkative or spoke faster than usual?

...thoughts raced through your head or you couldn't slow (your) mind down?

...you were so easily distracted by things around you that you had trouble concentrating or staying on track?

...you had much more energy than usual?

...you were much more active or did many more things than usual?

...you were much more social or outgoing than usual; for example, you telephoned friends in the middle of the night?

...you were much more interested in sex than usual?

...you did things that were unusual for you or that people might have thought were excessive, foolish, or risky?

...spending money got you or your family in trouble?

2. If you checked YES to more than one of the above, have several of these ever happened during the same period of time?

3. How much of a problem did any of these cause you – like being unable to work, having family, money, or legal troubles; getting into arguments or fights?

No Problem
Minor Problem
Moderate Problem
Serious Problem

Analysis

Each of the above listed questions was analyzed to determine if semantic choice and arrangement were culturally appropriate for the Hispanic patient and the extent to which it could have been misinterpreted by the patients (predictor variable) in such a way that it could have led to a misdiagnosis (outcome variable). The participants were asked to answer the questions and then expound on their personal interpretation of each question. Independent of their responses to each question, each participant was asked to describe, in their own words, what the question was asking. Their responses were listed below with the researcher's interpretation in an attempt to expose possible cultural misinterpretations.

Results

Listed below are the findings after the analysis of the MDQ, including interpretation of the specific questions by the researcher of the input provided by two voluntary participants (Respondent A and Respondent B). The respondents were asked to complete the MDQ and record their responses to each question. The respondents selected "YES" or "NO" to each of the questions based on their initial interpretation. After completion of the MDQ, the respondents were asked, independent of their responses, to describe what they believed to be the meaning of each question. Additionally, each question was analyzed by the researcher in English in an attempt to expose possible cultural misinterpretations as a result of semantic organization. It is important to note that neither Respondent A nor Respondent B, possessed an Axis I diagnosis of Bipolar I Mood Disorder.

1. Has there ever been a period of time when you were not your usual self and (while not on drugs or alcohol)

Respondent A – (YES) "Since I have been having problems with my wife, I feel depressed."

Respondent B – (NO) "If you were around other people who didn't know you, and they think you are weird."

Researcher's interpretation – The term "usual self" is problematic. What is considered "usual" or normal may have different cultural boundaries. The respondent may feel pressured to label what would be considered culturally normal behavior, as abnormal because of pressures in the testing environment.

2. You felt so good or so hyper that other people thought you were not your normal self or you were so hyper that you got into trouble?

Respondent A – (YES) "I answered yes, because people say I talk too much. When I worked the night shift (mostly Hispanic co-workers), I didn't have a problem, but they moved me to the morning shift (mostly Caucasian co-workers), they felt I talked too much."

Respondent B – (NO) "If I feel excited about something, people tell me to calm down."

Researcher's interpretation – The term "other people" could lead many Hispanic respondents to think of the Caucasian hegemony. From this perspective, their actions could be interpreted as abnormal.

3. You were so irritable that you shouted at people or started fights or arguments?

Respondent A – (YES) "My wife's brother comes over (to the house) without calling, and I get irritated."

Respondent B – (NO) "If people really bug me or won't leave me alone, I think about starting a fight."

Researcher's interpretation – Violence in the minority community is viewed much differently. Many Hispanics feel that "survival" in the barrio is dependent on being able to enter in and win physical confrontation.

4. You felt much more self-confident than usual?

Respondent A – (YES) "People say I need to take better care of myself (health), and that makes me more self confident."

Respondent B – (YES) "When I study for a test, I feel more confident."

Researcher's interpretation – In the Hispanic community, being confident or (seguro) is a positive trait. Respondents could be inclined to answer "YES" to this question based on cultural pressures promulgated by friends and family.

5. You got much less sleep than usual and found you didn't really miss it?

Respondent A – (NO) "I like to sleep."

Respondent B – (NO) "I can sleep anywhere."

Researcher's interpretation – Many Hispanics find themselves in a lower SES than Caucasians, stemming from limited employment opportunities. These jobs usually require working long hours which may interfere with sleep. Becoming accustomed to these patterns may result in a false positive answer for this question.

6. You were much more talkative or spoke faster than usual?

Respondent A – (YES) "I know I talk too much. I want to get it out quickly, because I know I'm going to get cut off."

Respondent B – (YES) "When I'm in a group or when talking with family in Spanish, I will talk faster than usual."

Researcher's interpretation – Many Hispanics who speak Spanish, find conversing with friends or family less intimidating than with strangers. In the home or with friends, many Hispanics will speak Spanish at a faster rate.

7. Thoughts raced through your head or you couldn't slow (your) mind down?

Respondent A – (YES) "It's like a test; I have to remember all the things in order so I don't get distracted. I have a lot on my mind."

Respondent B – (YES) "If I have so many things to do, and I know I have to get them done."

Researcher's interpretation – This could be interpreted with dealing with the problems of any minority experience. Discrimination and inequality lead to increased stress and cognitive momentum.

8. You were so easily distracted by things around you that you had trouble concentrating or staying on track?

Respondent A – (YES) "When I try to be with people, I get easily distracted by people around me."

Respondent B – (YES) "I feel that I get distracted when I try to study for a test."

Researcher's interpretation – From

a Hispanic cultural perspective in the U.S., much of which is affected by an external locus of control, a person could feel that external environmental stressors are in fact distracters.

9. You had much more energy than usual?

Respondent A – (NO) "I always feel tired if I don't get enough sleep."

Respondent B – (YES) "After working out, I feel that I have more energy."

Researcher's interpretation – In relation to question number 5, many Hispanics find that at the end of the day, they are physically exhausted. Having more energy than usual would be considered positive.

10. You were much more active or did many more things than usual?

Respondent A – (NO) "I sometimes prefer to stay at home and play video games or watch television."

Respondent B – (YES) "If I have a busy day at school or something like that."

Researcher's interpretation – This question could be interpreted as someone who has a lot to accomplish, and has responded accordingly.

11. You were much more social or outgoing than usual; for example, you telephoned friends in the middle of the night?

Respondent A – (NO) "I called my wife in the middle of the night to check on her, but everybody was still awake."

Respondent B – (YES) "If it's a holiday or if I have more time, or if I'm calling my family in Mexico."

Researcher's interpretation – In the Hispanic culture, siestas (late afternoon naps) are still widely practiced. It is not uncommon for a Hispanic to begin their evening much later, and stay out or awake until early hours of the morning.

12. You were much more interested in sex than usual?

Respondent A – (YES) "I feel that I am more interested in sex because I have problems related to my health condition. Also, sometimes I get interrupted when I am trying to have sex."

Respondent B – (YES) "Because of my age I am more interested in sex."

Researcher's interpretation – The concept of "macho" or masculine behavior is greatly regarded. A Hispanic male respondent will be much more inclined to answer "YES" to this question, as a "NO" response could be interpreted as a weakness in his masculinity.

13. You did things that were unusual for you or that people might have thought were excessive, foolish, or risky?

Respondent A – (YES) "Selling weed to family and friends is risky business and I shouldn't smoke weed because of my health."

Respondent B – (YES) "My family and parents always say that I do foolish things like drive too fast."

Researcher's interpretation – The term "coyote" in Spanish has multiple meanings. For many, it refers to the youngest boy in a family. The "coyote" is expected to engage in behaviors that could be considered more risky or foolish. Greater latitude is given to the "coyote" as he is considered the baby of the family.

14. Spending money got you or your family in trouble?

Respondent A – (YES) "I grew up poor, and never had money, so when I have money I like to buy things. My wife gets irritated when I buy things, and we have bills."

Respondent B – (NO) "I don't have any money to spend."

Researcher's interpretation – Many Hispanics in a lower SES, feel that "splurging" on non-essential items is a luxury. The typical "shopping spree" that this question focuses on is not applicable to many Hispanics.

15. If you checked YES to more than one of the above, have several of these

ever happened during the same period of time?

Respondent A – (YES) "I feel that many of the questions were related."

Respondent B – (NO) "Usually during different times."

Researcher's interpretation – Due to the design of many of these questions, it is likely that a Hispanic will answer "YES" to the majority of the questions, which increases the possibility that this latter question will also be answered "YES."

16. How much of a problem did any of these cause you – like being unable to work; having family, money, or legal troubles; getting into arguments or fights?

No Problem   Minor Problem   Moderate Problem   Serious Problem

Respondent A – (SERIOUS) "Everything that happens (in life) gets in the way, and I can't fix anything."

Respondent B – (MINOR PROBLEM) "I don't see any major problems."

Researcher's interpretation – This response to this question is very subjective to the interpretation of the previous questions. Respondents are likely to answer this question based on the preceding questions, which may have been misinterpreted.

Discussion

From the analysis of the MDQ and the responses by the participants, it can be concluded that this assessment tool is flawed in its design. Persons from different cultures may interpret the questions on the MDQ differently. The semantic design of the questions may lead Hispanic respondents to choose answers that are associated with the manic traits of the bipolar disorder. The findings of this project were consistent with the prediction that language and cultural differences in interpretation of the questions may result in improper diagnoses. The data collected presented false positives in all cases. It was concluded that the Mood Disorder Questionnaire is interpreted differently by Hispanic patients and could lead to a gross misdiagnosis. This may result in inappropriate treatment.

Additionally, the validation process of the MDQ did not include a representative percentage of Hispanics. The implications of the potential for misdiagnoses based on the interpretation of the MDQ are profound given the elevated rates of bipolar designation of Hispanics who are being medicated, and tracked into a system of care that is not relevant to their needs. For some, this pattern may represent a labeling process that could be associated with the further exacerbation of racism, discrimination, and inequality. Culturally inappropriate psychological testing has been associated with continued disparities in the mental heath field for Hispanics and other ethnic minorities.

A key example of how this assessment tool failed was observed by the researcher. A young Hispanic male was administered the MDQ, to which he answered "yes" to most all of the questions. Immediately, he was diagnosed as having bipolar disorder. It wasn't until further investigation that his misinterpretation of most of the questions on the MDQ was revealed. Unchanged, this patient would have carried this diagnosis of bipolar. It wasn't until his case was reevaluated that his Axis I diagnosis was corrected (Green, 2005). In cases such as this, patients become accustomed to their newly found "misdiagnosis," and learn to accept it. For him, a simple misinterpretation, could have led to a lifetime of inappropriate treatment.

During this investigation of the MDQ, the researcher noted that the development and validation of this psychological assessment tool was funded by a grant from Abbot-Bristol Meyers, GlaxoSmithKline, Organon, and Wyth-Ayerst, which are all leading manufacturers of mood stabilizing medications (Hirschfeld, et al., 2003). This finding poses question as to the motivation of the drug company's interest in the development of the MDQ. Independent of race or ethnic background, these drug manufacturers' actions may raise questions about their funding of an instrument that has the potential to increase diagnosis of bipolar cases and indirectly promote the use of their mood stabilizing medications.

If this trend is to be changed, more attention must be focused on the Hispanic patient. Specialized education must be developed to aid professionals working in this field in understanding the cultural anomalies that exist in the many Hispanic communities. New assessment tools, that are culturally relevant, must be created that identify psychological distress that is appropriately interpreted by the patient according to his or her culture. These tools must be available in English and Spanish to accommodate patients, despite their language. More programs that offer bilingual psychiatric care by Hispanic providers in a culturally inviting environment are needed to help to eliminate this disparity (Santiago-Irizzary, 1996). It should not be assumed that psychological assessment and treatment plans developed by and for the Caucasian will be applicable to all other races and ethnic groups. New programs must be developed that focus on Hispanic mental health within the community. Such programs have already been implemented by the Latino Behavioral Health Institute (LBHI). This past August the conference focused on "the elimination of discrimination against Latinos in need of behavioral health services related to Latino mental health, substance abuse, and health and human services" (LBHI, 2005). It will be through these kinds of efforts that the country can move toward a reduction in the noted disparities and a change in this regard will be realized for the Hispanic population of the United States.

The findings of this project were consistent with the hypothesized conclusion. The data collected presented false positives in all cases. It was concluded that the Mood Disorder Questionnaire is not culturally relevant to the Hispanic patient, and could lead to a gross misdiagnosis which may result in inappropriate treatment.

References

Burnam, A., Hough, R., Karno, M., Escobar, J., Telles. C. Acculturation and Lifetime Prevalence of Psychiatric Disorders Among Mexican Americans in Los Angeles. *Journal of Health and Social Behavior*.1987;28, 89-102.

Green, T. Critical Incident Journal Entry 7. University Hospital Psychiatry Unit. San Antonio, TX, 2005.

Hirschfeld, R. The Mood Disorder Questionnaire: A Simple, Patient-Rated Screening Instrument for Bipolar Disorder. Primary Care Companion Journal of Clinical Psychiatry. 2002; 4, 1.

Hirschfeld, R., Holzer, C., Calabrese, J., Weissman, M., Reed, M., Davies, M., et al. (2003). Validity of the Mood Disorder Questionnaire: A General Population Study. *American Journal of Psychiatry*. 2003;160, 178-180.

Hirschfeld, R., Williams, J., Spitzer, R., Calabrese, J., Flynn, L., Keck, P. Development and Validation of a Screening Instrument for Bipolar Spectrum Disorder: The Mood Disorder Questionnaire. *American*

Journal of Psychiatry. 2000;157, 1873-1875.

Kouyoumdjian, H., Zamboanga, B., Hansen, D. Barriers to Community Mental Health Services for Latinos: Treatment Considerations. *Clinical Psychology: Science And Practice*. 2003;10, 394-422.

Mirowsky, J., Ross, C. Mexican Culture and its Emotional Contradictions. *Journal of Health and Social Behavior*. 1984; 25, 2-13.

Rodriguez, A. (2005). Latino Behavioral Health Institute to Present Eleventh Annual Conference. Los Angeles, CA: LBHI, 2005.

Santiago, V. Culture as Cure. *Cultural Anthropology*. 1996;11, 3-24.

U.S. Census Bureau. General Demographic Characteristics: 2003 American Community Survey, 2003.

U.S. Department of Health and Human Services (DHHS). *Mental Health: A Report of the Surgeon General*. Rockville, MD: Author, 1999.

U.S. Department of Health and Human Services. *Mental Health Problems Among Minorities: Follow-up to Surgeon General's Report on Mental Health*. Rockville, MD: Author, 1999.

Giving Out Doses of Health

Tiffany Y. Jordan
Junior, Psychology

Dr. Debra L. Murphy, Major Advisor for Psychology

Abstract

This research reports on a qualitative analysis of educational/ informational sessions that were conducted in the author's capacity as a Consumer Health Advocate (CHA). This activity involved educating health consumers to use the National Library of Medicine (NLM) MedlinePLUS websites. Two to three months after being educated, half continued to use it, sixty percent (60%) told others about it and forty (40%) showed others how to use it. Through personal testimonials, some reported that even though they did not use the database themselves, they had told or shown someone else who they thought needed to use NLM, like a grandmother, mother, grandfather, and even their parents. This report focused on the observations that were made by the author of how the consumers reacted to the training sessions. Some of the young consumers (students) were not as interested as those who were older. The older consumers were more eager to learn about the website. Empowerment through teaching the community in need about how to access health information may be the key to life.

Keywords: consumer health advocate; National Library of Medicine; health disparities

*Funded by the National Library of Medicine and the Office of Minority Health

Introduction

This research is about the lack of information about health education, prevention, signs, and symptoms, diagnosis and treatment, and disease management getting to the population that is at the highest risk and educating them to obtain it. Getting health informational access education about the National Library of Medicine/ Medline Plus WEB data bases to those battling or at risk for AIDS, cancer, diabetes, and heart disease is the main focus of this author's role as a Consumer Health Advocate (CHA) through this university's Training and Education Grant Initiative which is funded by the Office of Minority Health and the National Library of Medicine. The NLM training is important because health disorders, such as, HIV/AIDS, diabetes, heart disease, and cancer are killing African Americans and Hispanics more than Whites.

The national level statistics show that African Americans and Hispanics are 40 percent higher than Whites when it comes to deaths of heart disease. African Americans and Hispanics are also 30 percent higher than Whites when it comes to deaths of cancer. African Americans and Hispanics have 7 times the deaths of that of Whites when it comes to HIV/AIDS (National Library of Medicine, 2006). The local level shows similar disparities.

One way that has been used to try to reduce these numbers of deaths is for Consumers Health Advocate (CHAs) who are certified through a Train the Trainer Masters Program to provide community consumers with education on how to access information from the NLM Website. Focus groups conducted in Austin and in the surrounding counties by Dr. Murphy's Huston-Tillotson University Biopsychosocial Aspects of Racial Disparities in Health class found that many individuals with these disparities or at risk for them reported not knowing how to prevent/ reduce these health disparities (Murphy, 2003). With the help of the training and education by CHAs, they were empowered with skills to access health information. Once educated, areas of interest to research included how they perceived and received the sessions in online access of health education and information, and whether or not they continued to use it, and how they use it.

Literature Review

There are over a hundred different websites on the Internet that showed up when health was entered as the search word. The main goal of all the websites is to prevent/reduce death disparities due to health. There are programs that are created to help those who are battling with diseases, to learn how to access health sites so that they can be informed about their conditions.

A study on people who have HIV/ AIDS showed that of 259 individuals, 51 percent had used the Internet and 59 percent had used the Internet to access health-related information. The majority of those who used the Internet for health-related and general purposes were better educated and had higher incomes than those who just used the Internet for general purposes. The study suggested that among Persons Living With HIV/AIDS (PLWA) individuals who access the Internet, particularly for health information, are among the healthier and more wealthy PLWAs (Kalichman, Benotsch, Weinhardt, Austin, and Luke,2002). This is one of the main reasons why the CHAs are doing training sessions on NLM, so that the lower income individuals can access information on how to live a healthier and better life. The gaps in the research include that there is a scarcity of qualitative information about how people react to being educated to access online health information. More needs to be known about: whether or not they use it; how those who use differ from those who do not use; how they use it; whether or not they are showing or telling others; who they are showing or telling; and how many they are showing or telling.

Method

A before and after design (pre-test and post-test) with the subject as its own control was conducted which included a focus on the collection of qualitative information (comments, body language, verbal and written comments) during the training and two to three months following it to ascertain whether or not those trained continued to use the skills that they learned. The cases included consumers from the campus and neighborhood clinics and other community based organizations who agreed to receive the online education. Fifty (50) cases were included in this paper. The answers from pre-post to post-test showed if learning had occurred and the consumers' responses presented evidence of whether or not they had used the education, why and how. Additionally, their body language and other comments provided information on their level of learning enthusiasm.

The education was conducted by trained and certified Student Consumer Health Advocates (CHAs). They targeted African Americans who are disproportionately suffering from health disparities. It. was done October 2005 to May 2006. The targeted area was the East Austin section of Austin, Texas. It occurred throughout the community and included churches, schools, community centers, and health fairs.

The CHAs started off the training session with a pre-test to see if the consumers knew anything about the NLM online data base; and if so how much. Once the pre-tests were completed, the CHAs educated the consumers about how to access NLM and the importance of NLM. The CHAs showed the consumers all the ways that accessing health information from the NLM data base can help to inform them and increase their knowledge and skills in online health information access with the hope that this would then assist them with preventing, reducing and coping with health issues. During the educational process, the CHAs also documented perceptions of how those taught responded to the education. After the educational session was completed, there was a post-test given to the consumers to see if they had learned how to use the NLM database and to get their perceptions about the educational session. Two (2) to-three (3) months after they had been trained their comments were recorded to see if they continued to use NLM, and to see whether or not they showed and/ or told other people about NLM.

The focus of this paper is to report on this author's qualitative analysis of consumers' perceptions and feedback that was gathered from those who were educated to shed information on whether or not they did or did not access the site and why or why not. Further, if they did use it, then how they used it was examined.

Percentages from the pre-test and posttest and the follow-up survey about whether or not they continued to use were compiled in the Statistical Package for the Social Sciences (SPSS) data base. There was also qualitative analysis of the researcher's observations of the consumers when they were educated. The observations that were made after each education at the neighborhood clinic and other sites were documented, plus the verbal feedback was recorded in writing. Analyses included examination of the themes that emerged from the documented body language observed and observations and comments that were recorded.

Results

Some consumers reported that they did not access the website because they were too busy or that they forgot the web address, or had no need for the website. Those responses mainly came from the younger consumers (college students). Some young consumers reported that they used it for an ill family member. They have also reported that the training and the site had helped them to improve their health behaviors.

The great majority of the results from the posttest were that they learned how to access NLM and that they planned to use the website, plus they felt empowered about their health and informed about the disparities of health in their community. While this was important, it was not the focus of this report, which is to provide qualitative information on the consumers' reactions to the training and why they did or did not continue to use it based on follow-up surveys. Half (50%) of the consumers continued to use NLM. Sixty (60%) told others about NLM and forty (40%) showed others how to use NLM. The focal point of this paper was on the qualitative information gathered about the consumers who received the education. The themes are reported below:

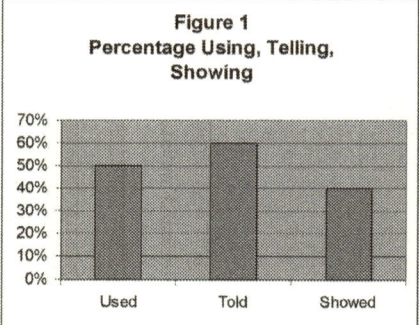

Figure 1
Percentage Using, Telling, Showing

- Younger consumers (students) tended to report that they used the information for school assignments and not for their own personal health reasons.
- Younger consumers were more likely than older consumers to report showing or telling someone else who needed it how to use.
- Grandparents, parents, and friends were the ones who the younger consumers reported telling or showing how to use NLM.
- Some of the younger consumers were not as engaged as the older consumers.
- The older consumers tended to be more focused, eager, willing to learn about the data base, and to be very hands-on with the trainers.

- The older consumers demonstrated a pattern of wanting to learn about all the links in the website
- The older consumers tended to be more likely to report feeling refreshed and empowered about their health after the education.
- The older consumers showed a pattern of wanting to learn how to use the site for information about their medications.
- The older consumers were eager to show and tell friends how to use the site.
- Overall, for all the consumers who were trained, they reported that the website was useful, whether they actually used the site on themselves or showed others.

Discussion

The problems that were found from the research were that some of the younger consumers did not use the skills that they learned in the session for themselves. Rather they used it for family members with health concerns or if they did use it, it was for classroom assignments. Some of the younger consumers were not as engaged with the session because they felt as if there was no need for it. This is consistent with literature research that the young tend toward feelings of invulnerability due to their age and that they are not getting these diseases as much as the older population. The CHAs are working to reform the training session to keep the younger consumers who may be bored more engaged in the session. It may need to be impressed upon them that being empowered about health is important because empowerment is the key to life.

The CHAs are working to have different training sessions for different age groups. This way the information is taught to everyone in a form in which they can understand and relate to it. What the younger consumers do not understand is that, the ages for all these health disparities occurring has been declining so that even those in elementary school are now developing diseases that are traditionally "middle age" disorders, such as, high blood pressure, diabetes, obesity, etc. So the younger consumers might not think that this database is for them, but it is for them. NLM is for everyone because it is to prevent/reduce health risks.

The overall training seems to be working. Even if half the consumers do not use NLM, they have shown someone else how to use it. So the knowledge is still being passed on to someone who does need it. Therefore, the training is not going to waste; the empowerment of life is still being spread.

References

Grossman, A.H., AIDS, HIV and at-risk youth: the myth of invulnerability. *Parks and Recreation.* 1991; 26; 11; 52-55; November, 1991.

Kalichman, S.C., Benotsch, G.E., Weinhardit, S. L., Austin, J., Luke. W. Internet use among people living with HIV/AIDS: association of health information, health behaviors, and health status *Education and Prevention.* 2002; *51-6*.

Murphy, D.L. Biopsychosocial Aspects of Racial Disparities in Health Course Findings, Huston-Tillotson University, Spring, 2005. Presented at the American Public Health Association Convention, December, 2006.

National Library of Medicine. Retrieved July 7, 2006. www.nlm.nih.gov/medlineplus/healthstatistics.html.

III. Abstracts of Literature Reviews

A Comparative Analysis of Health, Therapeutic, and Support Virtual Communities
to
Los Horcones

Alexander Anyaehie
Senior, Psychology

Dr. Debra L Murphy, Major Advisor for Psychology

This review compared and contrasted virtual communities with the communitarian society of Los Horcones, a Radical Behaviorist oriented community, and how Humanistic and Social Cognitive Theory can be related. In Los Horcones, behavioral engineering has been applied to try to achieve a better society. Elements of Social Cognitive and Humanistic Theory have also been applied. The similarities and differences of virtual communities compared with communitarian societies, such as, Los Horcones were examined and how they incorporate Radical Behaviorist, Humanistic, and Social Cognitive Theory into their approaches. Technology has made possible "virtual communities," which have many similarities to communitarian societies. Communitarian is defined as a society where members work together in cooperation toward the same objectives or ideals. Computer-mediated communication (CMC) is one of the new ways for humans to form social relations with one another, and it is growing rapidly. Through its six-week long dialogue with the Psychology Senior Seminar class, the Los Horcones Communitarian Society can be considered to have literally "morphed" itself into a virtual community with these HT students. Data and information were gathered from online resources, journals, and the biweekly online chat sessions that the Senior Seminar in Psychology Spring semester class of 2006 engaged in with the Los Horcones residents of Mexico. A recent survey of therapy/health and support group oriented virtual communities shows that consumer satisfaction with virtual communities is high, suggesting that the use of these vehicles will continue to grow in the future.

Symbolic Interactionism

Bassam Al-Mannai
Senior, Sociology

Dr. Rosalee Martin, Sociology Major Advisor

Symbolic interaction is a sociology theory based on the writings of Mead and Blummer. This presentation reviewed current perspectives on this theory and the Zimbardo prison experiment. The presentation included a history of the social theory and a discussion of the experiment.

Religious Diversity Leads to Tolerance*

Jiaoshu Zhang
Sophomore, Business Administration

Dr. James Kraft, Major Advisor for Religious Studies

Religious diversity leads to tolerance. Religious diversity enriches our lives, fosters epistemic humility, and aims at the same ultimate reality. First, religious diversity enriches us by sharing with each other. Diana Eck, one of the most well known scholars who talks about this topic, often has this approach. My colleague, Trent Reynolds thinks that religious diversity brings a negative influence and leads to intolerance. Confusion can not be blamed on religious diversity; instead it will enrich our arguments. Second, varied religious perspectives foster epistemic humility, which is Dr. Kraft's argument (when people become humble about what they believe they usually become more tolerant of the alternative perspectives). Dr. Koons argues people legitimately accept reports of religious experience immediately without needing to question it. The *prima facie* credibility of reports of religious experience is not applicable for most situations. Third, all faiths aim at the same ultimate reality even though they are limited and temporarily conflict with each other. John Hick states that all the religions are aiming at the same goal, the ultimate reality, though all approaches to it are limited. Adler thinks that two religions cannot both be correct if they are contradictory. Hick responds that the religious differences could be tolerated—especially when they are not the essential part of faith. Therefore, religious and philosophical diversity lead to tolerance.

*Abstract previously published [Zhang, Jiaoshu, Religious diversity leads to tolerance. *A Journal for Philosophy of Religion.* 2006; 26; 11; 52-55; November, 1991]

IV. Poster Session Abstracts

Primary Effects of ADDERALL® in the Human Body

Alexandra Aponte
Senior, Biology

Dr. Muchere Russ, Major Advisor for Chemistry

A drug widely distributed for the medical treatment of Attention Deficit Hyperactivity Disorder (ADHD) is commonly known as ADDERALL. This drug is a central nervous system stimulant composed of 4 main amphetamine salts. Amphetamines are thought to block the reuptake of norepinephrine and dopamine into the brain. The primary metabolic reactions of these salts were covered in this paper. There have been increasing reports of misuse of ADDERALL among young adults, particularly students. Additionally, amphetamines have been known to cause insomnia, irritability, hyperactivity, and personality changes. In severe cases, it has been also known to cause psychosis or even sudden death. Although the neurotoxic effects in humans are unknown, high doses of amphetamines were shown to produce nerve fiber damage in rodents. Several of the findings in these areas were covered in this report.

Analysis of the Photographic Portrayal of Female Athletes During the 2006 Winter Olympics

Natalia Portillo
Junior, Kinesiology

Dr. Rozena McCabe, Major Advisor for Kinesiology

Sixteen years after the passage of Title IX, the federal legislation which prohibits discrimination based on gender, Kane (1989) determined that female athletes were underrepresented in the media in comparison to their male counterparts. In addition, the female athletes who were in the media were portrayed in non-action poses and their femininity was emphasized. The purpose of this study was to determine if there was gender equality in the photographic portrayal of athletes during the 2006 winter Olympics within the Austin American-Statesman. Photographs of Winter Olympians published in the newspaper's sports section were tallied from Feb. 10th through Feb. 27th. Results indicated the percentage of photographs which portrayed female Olympians was 33%. Further analysis indicated that the depiction of the female athletes could be categorized as non-active, negative, and defeated in comparison to the males.

Non-Steroidal Anti-Inflammatory Drugs and Their Effects in Therapeutic Efficacy And Gastrointestinal Disorders

Alexander Rancier
Junior, Chemistry/Biology

Dr. Muchere Russ, Major Advisor for Chemistry

Nonsteroidal anti-inflammatory drugs (NSAIDs) are a group of compounds that serve as anti-inflammatory and analgesic agents. Some common effects of NSAIDs include many Gastrointestinal (GI) tract disorders. Much work has been done to study the mechanisms by which the analgesic and negative side effects of NSAIDs occur, so that newer compounds can be synthesized to increase therapeutic efficiency while lowering GI toxicity. The purpose of this experiment was to study a contingent of known NSAIDs (aspirin, ibuprofen, etc.) to examine their relative efficacy through in vivo assays, structural compositions, and chemical pathways. Furthermore, these compounds were compared to newly synthesized compounds to study their ability to be used as more effective NSAIDs.

Chemical Basis of Some Known Positive Effects of EGCG In The Human Body

Elizabeth Scott
Senior, Psychology

Dr. Muchere Russ, Major Advisor for Chemistry

For many years green tea has been used as an herbal remedy to prevent and to heal different ailments. The tea plant contains many kinds of polyphenols, especially catechins. The most abundant component of green tea (59.1%) is the catechin, (-)-Epigallocatechin gallate, also known as EGCG. EGCG has been shown to cause a different oxidative environment in malignant versus normal epithelial cells. Studies showed that EGCG can be used with cancer treatments to help stop the growth of cancer cells. Green tea polyphenols are considered beneficial to human health, especially as cancer preventive agents.

Compound Caffeine: Antagonist by Nature

W. Twelvis Matthews
Junior, Biology

Dr. Muchere Russ, Major Advisor for Chemistry

The primary purpose of this study was to elucidate and characterize the function of antagonist caffeine, agonist adenosine, and the adenosine receptor systems thereof based upon early pharmacological and present genetic studies.

Special Acknowledgements:

The students who participated in Research Day
Dr. Joseph Jones, Dean of Arts and Sciences, who initiated Research Day

The Huston-Tillotson University Inaugural
Student Research Day Committee
Dr. Muchere Russ, Chair
Dr. Debra L. Murphy, Journal Editor
Mr. Eric Budd
Dr. Vanessa L. Davis
Dr. Joseph Jones, ex officio

Advisors for Student Publications
Biology and Chemistry, Dr. Muchere Russ
Business Administration, Dr. Robert Kellogg
Kinesiology, Dr. Rozena McCabe
Psychology, Dr. Debra L. Murphy
Religious Studies, Dr. James Kraft
Sociology, Dr. Rosalee Martin

Supported by:

The UNCF SEEDS Grant Natural Sciences and Mathematics Department (Dr. Kathy Schwab, Principal Investigator/Project Director)

The Office of Minority Health (OMH) Grant, Psychology (Social Sciences Department) (Dr. Debra L. Murphy, Principal Investigator/Project Director)

www.ingramcontent.com/pod-product-compliance
Lightning Source LLC
Chambersburg PA
CBHW021240280526
45784CB00005B/2172